Francis William Pitt Greenwood

Sermons of Consolation

A New Edition

Francis William Pitt Greenwood

Sermons of Consolation
A New Edition

ISBN/EAN: 9783744745031

Printed in Europe, USA, Canada, Australia, Japan

Cover: Foto ©Lupo / pixelio.de

More available books at **www.hansebooks.com**

SERMONS OF CONSOLATION.

BY
F. W. P. GREENWOOD, D. D.,
LATE MINISTER OF KING'S CHAPEL, BOSTON.

A NEW EDITION.

BOSTON:
LITTLE, BROWN AND COMPANY.
1864.

PREFACE.

I HAVE been induced to publish a volume of sermons chiefly by the desire of being yet heard by the people of my ministry, though withheld by the hand of Providence from addressing or meeting them in the church. But I will not deny that with this desire was mingled the hope that the volume might be received with favor, and do some service, beyond the bounds of my parish.

The tone and character of the sermons has been determined by the conviction I have entertained, in common with many of my brethren, that a great dearth existed of books of a consolatory character, such as are earnestly sought for by mourners in the days of their mourning, and are suitable to be placed in their hands. Although the deficiency has of late been partly supplied by one or two useful compilations, I am acquainted with no volume of sermons devoted to the single purpose of consolation. If there be such a volume, it has not come into use among us.

But while I have given my collection of discourses unity by restricting it to this one object, I am conscious that I have at the same time exposed it to the charge of containing repetitions, not of thought only, but of phrase. Repetitions, doubtless, there are; but I know not how they could easily have been avoided, and I trust they will not prove tiresome. The discourses were written separately, at distant intervals, and with no idea, at the time, that they would ever be brought together. Moreover, the great sources of consolation are but few, and remain the same from year to year and age to age, because they are sufficient for their end and for our condition. Not being able to avoid repetition entirely, I have, however, obviated the difficulty, as far as possible, by introducing a large variety of topics within the prescribed limits,—the end being always that of consolation.

The date which is printed at the end of each sermon denotes the time when it was first preached. I have done this, which in itself can be of no inconvenience to the reader, merely for the sake of my own private reference.

F. W. P. G.

November 1, 1842.

CONTENTS.

SERMON I.
Sorrow and Joy . . . .

SERMON II.
God Incomprehensible . . .

SERMON III.
God All-Powerful . . .

SERMON IV.
God the Guardian of Souls .

SERMON V.
Folly of Atheism . . .

SERMON VI.
Dwelling in the Temple . .

SERMON VII.
Death an Appointment 71

SERMON VIII.
The Time of Death 80

SERMON IX.
The House of Mourning 94

SERMON X.
Consolations of Religion 105

SERMON XI.
Blessing God in Bereavement 117

SERMON XII.
Remembrance of the Righteous 128

SERMON XIII.
Nothing without Christ 138

SERMON XIV.
Perpetuity of Christ's Kingdom . . . 151

SERMON XV.
Independence on Human Sympathy . . . 164

CONTENTS.

SERMON XVI.
Christ our Fellow-Sufferer

SERMON XVII.
Seeing the Departed

SERMON XVIII.
The Crown of Thorns

SERMON XIX.
Recognition of Friends

SERMON XX.
Voices from Heaven

SERMON XXI.
The Good Revealed

SERMON XXII.
Walking by Faith

SERMON XXIII.
Lessons of Autumn

SERMON XXIV.
It is Well

SERMON XXV.

OFFICES OF MEMORY . . . .

SERMON XXVI.

PEACEFUL SLEEP . . . . .

SERMON XXVII.

CHRIST WITH US AT EVENING . .

SERMONS.

SERMON I.

SORROW AND JOY.

Is any among you afflicted? Let him pray. Is any merry? Let him sing psalms. — *James* v. 13.

Much of the experience, which is also intended to be the discipline of life, is divided between its sorrows and its joys. It is the counsel of the apostle James, that the sentiments and principles of religion should be present with their holy influences in both of these conditions. He would have us sanctify our troubles and our pleasures by thoughts of Him who appoints them. Whether the heart be depressed by grief or elated by gladness, let it be placed under the wise care of piety, so that it may be neither sunk too low nor raised too high, but always kept within the sphere of duty, and near unto God. It must be so instructed, that it may pour out its fulness in supplication or in praise, and not suffer the wealth of its deep fountains to run to waste.

Some hearts are guided, and some are not, by the spirit of our text; and mankind might almost be classed, with regard to religious character, by the different ways in which they entertain sorrow and joy. In determining for ourselves the great question, whether we are living under the law of God or not, whether we are guided and governed by his voice or not, whether we reverently regard his will or not, we can have no better criterion than the manner in which we find ourselves affected by the chastenings and the mercies, by the dark and the bright dispensations of his Providence. In determining the same question, also, concerning others, so far as we are permitted to determine it, that is to say, in forming those opinions of general and individual character, which observation and intercourse oblige and require us to form, but which should always be directed by the utmost fairness and the gentlest charity, the same criterion may be applied, only with far more caution and tenderness in the case of others than in our own. What we know of ourselves will assist us in our observation of others; what we see of others will aid us in the examination of ourselves. But it is ourselves whom we should search the most thoroughly and judge the most strictly. It is ourselves of whom we should learn the most, know the most, and exact the most.

How then is it with us in those two opposite conditions of existence to which our text refers? How is it with our own souls, when they are overwhelmed by sorrow, and when they are illumined by joy? To which class do we belong? to those who regard, or those who disregard the counsel of the apostle?

To consider, first, the condition which is first mentioned in the text, how is it with our souls in sorrow? How are they affected? How do they demean themselves? Where do they look? What is their language? When we are afflicted, do we pray? Do we go for comfort to the Comforter? Do we lay the burden of our woes at the feet of our Father? Do we sympathize with the spirit of the Psalmist when he says, "Be merciful unto me, O God, be merciful unto me, for my soul trusteth in thee; and under the shadow of thy wings shall be my refuge, until this calamity be overpast?" Do we regard adversities as the sober angels of God, sent from him and leading to him; or, on the other hand, as if affliction came forth from the ground, do we rest our regards upon the ground, and cast upwards not a glance, not a hope, not the least whispering of a prayer? Are we never brought before the footstool of the Almighty but by some signal misfortune, some strong and irresistible grief, and only then to cry out in terror or impatience, and pray to be delivered from trouble, without praying for submission, and strength to bear it? If this is all our prayer, we do not pray. There is no faith, no humility, no resignation in such a cry. It is complaint, not prayer. We are among the worldly. We have yet to learn the nature and to experience the power of true religion.

Let us look for a moment about us, and observe how sorrows are entertained by the mass of mankind. If they are afflicted, do they pray? Far from it. I do not mean that it is necessary they should pray aloud in affliction, and before the presence of men. Nor would such praying, of itself and unaccompanied by other manifestations, prove that they prayed. But their manners, their language, their conduct, show plainly that they do not pray; that the spirit within them does not pray; that they do not bow themselves down in humble supplication before Him who chastens them. They do not look beyond the mere event, the loss, the disappointment, the pain, the care, or whatever else the immediate occasion of their grief may be. They do not attempt to raise themselves above it. They are the slaves of circumstance. They talk of fate. They murmur at their destiny. They blindly submit to a blind fortune, or as blindly struggle and fight against it.

One man is irritated by adversity. He takes no pains to conceal his vexation. The gloom of night is under his brows. He speaks as if he had suffered some sore injustice. He cannot specify any individual who has wronged him, but conceives himself wronged in some way by the event itself, which causes his affliction; and as he cannot make the event feel any retaliation, he vents his moroseness in the ears or to the eyes of all who approach him. He is voluble of his vain and wearying complaints, or he chills and darkens the surrounding atmosphere by his stern and forbidding aspect.

Another man is not irritated by adversity, or at least he does not openly show that he is irritated. He endures misfortune, bereavement, pain. But what endurance! hard, cold, proud, or reckless. What endurance! turning away from thought, ignorant of the ministry of hope, fastened to the cheerless present, holding no converse with the invisible and the future. What endurance! stiffening and cramping, not supporting the soul. It speaks the sufferer's mind as plainly as words could speak, and says, " There! it has come, and I must bear it; it is done, and cannot be undone. The harsh commands of fate are issued, and, as I cannot resist, I have nothing to do but submit to them. As I cannot cure the ills of fortune, the world shall see that I can endure them. I will not complain; for what is the use of complaining? I cannot help what has happened, and why should I trouble myself about it?" This is his endurance; and this is all the use which he sees fit to make of the moral strength and spiritual capacities with which God has endowed him, and of the lessons which God has sent him. He has a soul, as if he had it not. He has a soul, made in the likeness of its Creator, and he seems as unmindful of that divine affinity as if it had been made by chance, in the likeness of chance, and under the absolute dominion of chance.

The way in which joy is received and appreciated by the multitude is not in its nature different from their entertainment of sorrow. It shows the same shallowness, the same want of reflection and hope and elevation, the same confinement to the present, the same dependence on circumstance. The joy of one will be noisy and boisterous, while that of another will run in a gentler, though not a deeper stream. Both are derived from casual sources, flow but a short distance, and are soon dried up. There is enough of mirth among men, but very little pious mirth. The spirit which is made glad by the mercies of God, singeth no psalms to his praise and giveth no glory to his name. It heedeth not the Psalmist's injunction, " Praise the Lord, O my soul, and forget not all his benefits." It was never mindful of those benefits, and therefore cannot even forget them. Its music has no rich chords of grateful feeling, but is light and fugitive; a song of earth, transient as dew, but not, like the dew, rising to heaven. There is no heart in such joy. It sends forth no pulses of life, no permanent influences. It is a sentiment which looks not beyond the occasion which gave it birth, and remains not when the occasion is gone. He, by whom it is experienced, is not carried by it beyond its own immediate precincts. He rests in the mere event. He takes the blessing which descends to him from above, as if he had found it or bought it; as if it were entirely his own, his own to use as he pleases, to abuse if he pleases. He receives, but considers not that there is One who bestows. He enjoys, but his heart is made no holier, nor more peaceful by his happiness. He is merry, but no psalm of thanksgiving tells of his gladness or perpetuates its memory; no incense of sweet savor is burnt on the cold and unvisited altar of the temple within.

Am I at all unjust in these delineations? Are not the joys and the sorrows of many thus borne, thus appreciated? If I am right so far, then the conclusion follows inevitably, that this number are either without religion, or that their religion is for the most part nominal and without efficacy. Some make no pretensions to religion. They neither have nor claim to have it. Are we content to be numbered among them? God grant that we may not be. But if we are not, we must necessarily fall into the class of those whose religion is lifeless and inefficient, if our sorrow is prayerless and the hymn of our joy rises not to heaven. This is a test from the certainty of which we need not strive to free ourselves by any sophistry; for there is no such thing as eluding it. If in adversity we are murmuring and despairing, or rigid and obstinate; if in prosperity we congratulate ourselves without thanking our Maker or even thinking of him; if the occasions of grief and gladness do not both lead us into his presence and unite us to him with increasing closeness, we may be sure that our religion is sadly deficient, that it is little more than a name, and that we are very far from the kingdom of God.

But who is he in whose heart the principles of religion have been carefully, tenderly fostered, and on whose conduct and life they exercise their proper energies, and to whose character they yield their natural fruits? We may know him by his deportment in the day of tribulation and anguish, and in the day of prosperity and rejoicing; and if we can see in our own deportment any good correspondence to his, we have a fair ground for concluding that our hearts and lives are regulated by the same influences, that we have some true knowledge of religion, some practical experience of its supporting and sanctifying power. In affliction he prays. He needs not to be directly reminded of the apostle's counsel. He goes easily and naturally, and by an inward prompting, to his heavenly Father, and unbosoms his griefs before him. He waits not for other consolations, but looks immediately to the grace of God, saying, " O God, thou art my God; early will I seek thee." "From the ends of the earth will I call upon thee, when my heart is in heaviness." The answer of his prayer is peace. There is peace on his countenance, peace in his gentle words, peace in his kind deportment, because peace has come down from God, whose only gift it is, and has taken up its abode in his quiet and trusting soul. You may witness his sadness, you may see his tears; but his sadness wears no despairing or repulsive guise, and there is no unbecoming passion in his tears. He complains not of fate, for he acknowledges no such power. He neither reviles nor submits to fortune, for he worships not fortune, but the eternal and unchangeable God. How soft is his sorrow, and how it softens without distressing others!

And how harmless, how childlike, how grateful is his joy! How careful is he not to let it run to riot, and spend itself in vain dissipation. The song of his gladness is a psalm of gratitude, the echoes of which may be heard from every object around him. He sympathizes with all the innocent joy on the earth, but he remembers that all this joy has a source; and as before in sorrow, so now in delight, he looks beyond earth and earthly things. He regarded affliction as sent, and he prayed and was resigned. He regards his happiness as given, and he is grateful, and seeks to impart of his abundance, and make others happy and cheerful and grateful.

"His fine-toned heart, like the harp of the winds,
 Answers in sweetness each breeze that sings;
And the storm of grief, and the breath of joy,
 Draw nothing but music from its strings."

Is this the manner in which we receive the impressions of sorrow and joy? Are we free from temporal bonds and the authority of passing things? Is it our custom to rise above the shadows of earth into the light of heaven? Do we get out from the thraldom of mere events, and regard what is beyond and above these events? In these two great conditions of life, the sad and the joyful conditions, do we acknowledge a Supreme Disposer, and connect ourselves with him, and feel and act as under his disposal? If so, then we are not strangers to religion. We are in the right way, the way of life, and, without doubt or mistrust, should use the best of our diligence to press onward in the same. Doubt and mistrust belong only to those who have not made religion their own, by a practical and close application of its principles to the conditions of their life. They may have professed religion, and may have thought, with entire sincerity, that religion was no stranger to them. But they have not made it their own, unless they have experienced its instructing and sustaining power; unless it has taught them to pray and to sing. It really abides with those alone within whom it effectually works. They who have experienced its help and operation within them cannot doubt of its presence, and cannot mistrust its character. It is not with them a matter of profession only, but of conviction. They do not doubt, because they know. They are not distracted between this and that opinion or form, but they go on in the path which they have felt to be that of truth and salvation, because in it they have met with strength and health and joy. They do not stop or hesitate, but they go steadfastly onwards, praying always in the spirit, and making melody in their hearts unto God.

MARCH 24, 1833.

SERMON II.

GOD INCOMPREHENSIBLE.

Behold, I go forward, but he is not there; and backward, but I cannot perceive him; on the left hand, where he doth work, but I cannot behold him; he hideth himself on the right hand, that I cannot see him. — *Job* xxiii. 8.

The God whom we worship is incomprehensible. The Being whom we are required to serve is not subject to the apprehension of any of our senses. The Spirit, holy, uncreate, and eternal, whom the heart should love supremely, and the mind must reverence with an awful fear, cannot be grasped by the spirit of man. The stream perceives not its fountain; the creature understands not its Creator. Many things we know, but we know not him who knows us best, — far better than we know ourselves. Our faculties make their little progresses from infancy to maturity; the human intellect enlarges by painful additions the field of its exercise; and the stores of knowledge receive a slow and fluctuating increase from age to age; but the Source of all intelligence is not found out to perfection,— the depths of the Divine Mind remain unfathomed. We may go forward; we may pierce, as far as our sight will permit us, into the uncertain void of futurity; from the accumulated heights of what we have done, we may look out on the shadowy and misty scene of what we may do,— but He is not there; there is no promise in our nature which leads us to hope for a clearer discernment on earth of the nature of God. We may go backward, far back among the monuments and opinions and great names of remotest antiquity, but there we cannot perceive him, there we find no knowledge of him greater than our own. The lights of antiquity shed no brightness, the sages are confounded, and the oracles are dumb. We may turn to the right hand and to the left, and though we are surrounded by the works, we cannot behold the Maker; we see beauty and order, and we infer that the Cause must be wise; we see magnificence and sublimity, and we know that the Cause is great; happiness, and we call it merciful and good; but that which is thus wise and great and good we cannot see. He hideth himself, so that we cannot perceive him.

God is incomprehensible in two principal respects: in his nature, and in the ways of his providence; in the modes of his existence, and the modes of his government.

He is *invisible*, and on that account incomprehensible. No man hath seen God at any time, nor can see him; it is not given to us to look upon his face and live. We know that he must be about us, wherever we are; but that he is so, is a deduction of reason, and not an intimation of sense. Whatever is invisible must be unknown in all those respects in which sight contributes to knowledge. Definiteness at least is wanting to our perceptions. Form is absent, and there is no ground for experiment or investigation. In another state of being, it is possible that Deity may be perceived without being seen, but in this mortal life the intervention of the senses is necessary to the satisfaction of our inquiries; and that of which they can take no cognizance is always, to a certain extent, incomprehensible, if it be of the nature of substantial existence.

God is incomprehensible, secondly, because he is *eternal;* and of eternity itself we can form no adequate conception. That this is an attribute of Deity is a plain conclusion of reason; and yet, that which our reason tells us must be, is not in itself to be comprehended by reason. It must be that everything which does or ever did exist should be brought into existence by some cause; and it must be that the cause of everything else is itself uncaused, independent, without beginning, and without end. What thoughts are these! They can hardly be called thoughts,—they are without form and void, like chaos,—they call for the brooding inspiration of the Creator himself, in some distant and high exalted state of our now infant being, to reduce them into order and distinctness, and pronounce over them the incommunicable will, Let there be light. And yet, that the first Cause could ever begin to exist, or that there ever was a time, go back as far as you will, before which there was no time, is, I will not say inconceivable, but unreasonable and absurd. There must have been time, antecedent to any supposed time; and that time must have been an eternity; and coeval with that unimaginable eternity must have been the existence of the great First Cause, the eternal, immortal, invisible God,— God the uncreated and the incomprehensible. To escape, therefore, from an absurdity, the tired and feeble thought is forced to take refuge and rest from its baffled flight in that which is incomprehensible. Truly, he hideth himself from the search of our slow and partial faculties, and we cannot see him.

Again; God is incomprehensible because he is *omnipotent* and *infinite*. He fills all space, as well as all time; inhabits both immensity and eternity; is endless and boundless. Equally present throughout his vast dominions, he lives and reigns, absolute and unapproachable. In the calm silence of a starry night, we look up to the myriads of worlds which adore God in their brightness; we calculate with time and pains the distance of one of these from the spot on which we stand, and the result seems like a fable, and overwhelms us with astonishment. By artificial aids to our sight, new sparkles of heavenly fire emerge into the field of vision, as distant from those we last saw as they from us. We borrow augmented assistance, and dim and struggling spots of light appear, — worlds, doubtless, and systems of worlds, but remote from us beyond the power of science to compute their remoteness, far away in the unknown deep, with their own fair brotherhood around them. Yet what is this? What is this incalculable reach of nature's trebled vision, but a glimpse into the thin suburbs of creation; an uncertain and unsatisfactory glance upon the sentinels and outposts merely of that host of heaven and army of God which stretch their numberless ranks beyond? And there, too, in the midst, all around, is God, to uphold what he has created, to regulate what he has ordained. And how can we perceive, how can we know the Maker, when we see but a small fragment only of the works, throughout the whole of which he dwells invisible?

Neither are our ideas capable of rising to the summits of God's power and wisdom. We know that these must be as infinite as the universe; that they must be equal to every demand which has been or may be made on their exertion, by boundless space and endless time, and a varied and mighty creation. How the same Hand which holds and balances all worlds should also give to every bird its plumage, and every blade of grass its hidden texture, and every insect its invisibly minute and yet perfect economy; and how the same Mind which orders the motions of the planets, and regulates the seasons, and commands the lightnings, and weighs the proportions of the atmosphere, should also note each sparrow which falls to the ground, and number all the hairs of our heads, is something which we may distantly admire, and yet endeavor to reach in vain. It is knowledge too high for us, and we cannot attain unto it.

Thus we see it follow, even from what we are said to know of God, and what in a limited sense indeed we do know, that he is not to be known with intimacy; that we cannot perceive him; that he is incomprehensible. And let it not be intimated that the foregoing remarks are mere speculations. They are speculations truly, but not mere or useless speculations, if they help to induce us to bow before the Supreme Spirit with a reverential awe, and to abase our own spirits into their humble and proper domains. For at the same time that the majesty and greatness of God are set forth by the incomprehensibleness of his nature, the weakness of our own nature is manifested, which is unable to comprehend him.

But though we have attended to the mysteries of God's existence, we have not yet spoken of the wonders of his ways and the dispensations of his providence. Here, too, he is incomprehensible. We stand and contemplate the only world of whose affairs we have any knowledge, a world in which evil is mixed in large proportions with good, and we are prompted to ask why this is so. Why are the resistless elements convulsed out of their peaceful duties into angry and fearful contention? Or, if they must sometimes breathe their energies in battle, why must earth be desolated, and earth's inhabitants be mournfully swept away in the struggle? And, far worse than any physical evil or disorder, why is sin permitted to enter the bowers of innocence and blight its blossoms; to exercise dominion over the soul of man, and often to reduce it into hopeless slavery? We see the proud sinner triumph; we see the righteous man distressed. We are made to know that, from the first instant of its being, human flesh is the weeping heir of unnumbered ills. Diseases lay waiting in disregarded ambush, and rush out upon us with deathful strength. The grass can hardly grow over a domestic tomb, before the turf is broken up to admit a new deposit beneath it. Nor is this all. The single, the unconnected, the apparently useless, who care for none and for whom no one cares, live on into shaking age and a second childhood; while the son, who by his manly exertions placed himself as a staff in the hands of his parents, is suddenly struck from under them; or the parent, on whom a young family depended for support, advice, instruction, sympathy, is removed by a dark, a seemingly midnight destiny, from their presence, and the orphans are left to wander on alone through the uncertain fortunes of the world.

We are troubled in our hearts at these things, and say that they are obscure and unaccountable, and that we do not understand them. How should we understand them? That these seeming disorders sometimes produce evident good cannot be denied, and then we perceive their heavenly purposes; but why is it wonderful, or why should we be troubled, that in many cases we cannot comprehend them, while we so feebly and imperfectly comprehend the Being who directs them? When we can see the whole plan of universal government spread out plainly before us; when we are acquainted with all that is done in each orb of creation, and with all the connections between each other orb and our own; when all space unrolls itself like a scroll to our vision; when the acts of time past and the secrets of time to come are made present to our watching mind; when we can behold the end from the beginning, and trace all the relations and dependencies between the beginning and the end; when we can do this, or but a part of this, then shall we be fitted to perceive how light springs up from darkness, and order from confusion, and good from ill; how imperfection ministers to perfection, accident to certainty, weakness to greatness, and temporal sorrow to everlasting bliss;—but till then, let us be humble in our ignorance and confiding in our devotion; let us be satisfied that he who knows all things completely will order all things wisely; and that we who cannot comprehend his ways ought not to elevate our blindness into the judgment-seat over them.

Let us only confine ourselves to ourselves. Let us consider how little we know of our own structure and composition; how baffled we are in our endeavors to unravel the delicate web of thought; how small our authority is over our condition; how ignorant we are of our lot, and how uncertain of our life, and how circumscribed in our mortal course. Then let us reflect that the Maker knows us, who are his workmanship, more thoroughly than the potter knows the vessel which he turns off from his wheel. Let us reflect, also, that with all his creatures, in all his worlds, he is equally as well acquainted as he is with us. Then let us again attempt to go through the marvellous extent of his creation, and again try to conceive of a God who sees it all, at every moment, with one glance of his omniscience, and governs it all in the ubiquity and plenitude of his wisdom, and we shall be convinced how inadequate we are to enter further than he may give us leave into the unsounded abyss of his counsels. "For his thoughts are not our thoughts, neither are our ways his ways; for as the heavens are higher than the earth, so are his ways higher than our ways, and his thoughts than our thoughts." Our minds are indeed the inspiration of the Almighty, but shall they lift themselves up to cope with the exhaustless source which inspired them? Shall they convert their divine relationship into presumption, and pretend to scan aright the stores and treasures of their great Original? Oh no!

"Reason's brightest spark,
Though kindled by thy light, in vain would try
To trace thy counsels, infinite and dark;
And thought is lost ere thought can soar so high."

But here we again go back, and find in what amazes and awes our souls their chief comfort and consolation. It is because God is so great that we cannot comprehend him; and yet if he were not so great, we could not rely on him with that security of trust which is our reasonable tribute to perfection. Our ignorance here becomes, in a high and important sense, our bliss. If it were so, that, with our present constitution and powers, born of the dust, and doomed to return to the dust again, we could nevertheless understand fully the nature of the Supreme, and make ourselves masters of his will, would not the circumstance argue his finiteness and imperfection, and diminish both our veneration and our confidence? But with respect to the eternal, all-seeing, and all-pervading Deity, this cannot be so. We cannot comprehend him. To know this, is to know enough; for the very reason why we know no more is the reason why our dependence should be absolute and fearless. Weakness cannot comprehend Omnipotence, but it can lean upon it securely; the finite cannot measure the Infinite, but it can resign itself cheerfully and unreservedly to its disposal. Let us make, therefore, a wise use of our ignorance; let the cause of doubt be the origin of confidence, and confusion and amazement subside into submission and quietness.

Yet more we are permitted to know, for our encouragement, in the Gospel of Christ; to know that not eternal wisdom alone, but infinite and impartial love presides over the universe; that we are in the hands of a Father, who, with more than an earthly parent's tenderness and solicitude, provides for the wants and hearkens to the cries of all his children. It is revealed to us, moreover, that as our knowledge so our very being also is in its infancy; that in a future state of being our knowledge will be active and progressive; new light poured upon its way, new energy given to its wings; that much which here has seemed dark will there be made plain; that God will manifest himself more fully to our comprehension; and that love will rise with rising intelligence, forever glowing and increasing in the presence of God, and the fulness of joy which is at his right hand.

OCTOBER 1, 1826.

SERMON III.

GOD ALL-POWERFUL.

God hath spoken once: twice have I heard this; that power belongeth unto God. — *Psalm* lxii. 11.

When the mind goes forth amidst the works of nature and the broad ranges of the universe, the first impression which it receives is that of power. Things are presented to it in grand masses, and it is not till after some time that it contracts itself to examine them in detail. Everywhere about us there is height, and depth, and expanse, and grandeur, and fulness; and of all these, power is the ever-present and ever-speaking attribute. The sky with its all-enclosing dome; the splendid sun; the glittering company of stars; the sweeping clouds; the broad-based, solemn mountains; the far off horizon; the wide, resounding sea, wear the constant expression of power. All the most common and apparent things, which the most directly and incessantly press upon our notice, are the most vast and powerful. Beside the objects already mentioned, there is space which is boundless, and time which is incessant and endless, and the air which wraps up the globe of the world, with all its inhabitants and contents, all proclaiming the word of power, and exciting the idea of power.

But whose power is it? for we perceive not only power but designing power. Where did it come from? for when we look on the great streams, we inquire for their source. Who can go out in the hushed and serious time of night, and raise his regards to the spangled firmament, with the knowledge that each point of light there is a ponderous world, steadfast in itself and in its relations to the great whole, and that those of them which are moving are moving with a velocity which confounds thought, and yet with a certainty of revolution which can be calculated to a second; who, when the winds are abroad, making the ocean to rage mightily, can view the tumult from the shore, conscious of his own safety, and that bounds are appointed to the threatening waves which they cannot pass; who can observe the travelling clouds pouring out their showers as they are needed upon the grateful earth; who can mark the seasons as they come round in punctual and yet ever-varying return;—who can see and understand such things, and refuse entrance to the conviction that they were intended; that there is a purpose at work in them and over them; that these operations are directed by some intelligent existence; that there is some controlling and designing being to whom all this power belongs?

"It belongs to the things themselves," is the discordant cry of a few, and happily but of a few. "The power is in the machine itself. The universe is god, — its own god. Why pretend to look further than you can see? Use your senses, which are the only means of knowledge. Be not superstitious, and concern not yourself about a being who does not exist, because the senses do not apprehend him." Well, then, I will use my senses, since that is the word. I will go to them obsequiously, and implore them to let me know where the intelligence is whose designs are everywhere around me. They can tell me nothing. I look, and I see nothing; I hearken, and I hear nothing; I reach forth my hands, and I feel nothing, in the whole congregation of material existences, which appears to me to possess mind and intelligence of itself. In the clods beneath me I perceive no self-governing wisdom; in the stars above me I perceive no spirit of order; in the waves of ocean I am apprised of no ruling mind. I see, I hear, I feel nothing in matter, like a planning, organizing, directing principle; and that is the very reason why I believe that there is such a principle, or Being, separate from matter, and superior to it. For one thing I do perceive, and that is design; of one thing I am certain, and that is, that there is somewhere a mind intently at work; the proofs of intention are too plain to be mistaken; and therefore when I use my senses, as I am requested to do, and receive no information from them that matter can rule itself, I form the direct conclusion from this silence and negative evidence of my senses, that there is a Being, a Supreme Being who rules it; for sure I am that it is ruled. I will not be so superstitious, therefore, as to believe in the contradiction of an unintelligent system acting of itself intelligently. I am advised not to be credulous. I will not be. I will admit nothing but on fair proof. Because my senses show me no visible, audible, tangible intelligence, I shall not therefore believe that there is no intelligence, but the very reverse, that there is one; one whom the senses cannot show me, one whom I cannot see, nor hear, nor feel, except in the wise and beautiful order of the universe and in the beatings of my heart; one who is invisible, inaudible, intangible, but to the eye of my mind, and the ear of my spirit, and the demonstrations of my reason. In following my senses, therefore, I am brought to my God; because they show me design, and cannot show me the designer. Now it is that the dumb works of nature break their silence, and utter speech of their Creator and of mine. Now it is that the mountains echo to the sea, and earth repeats to heaven, the holy name of Him who ordains their order and rules their motions. Now it is that their voice becomes the voice of God himself, proclaiming and reiterating his divine supremacy. "God hath spoken once; twice have I heard this; that power belongeth unto God."

But it is not in the surrounding universe alone that the believer perceives the power of God. He delights to trace it throughout the course of his own being, and in all that concerns his own government and welfare and the lives and welfare of his brethren.

I. He sees this power, in the first place, in his life. What but almighty power brought him into existence? What but almighty power is equal to the creation of a living soul? What but the breath of the Original Spirit could breathe into us, or anything, the breath of life. We are used to go about carelessly, and eat and drink, and pursue our business or pleasure, and hold converse with our friends and the world, without reflecting on the exertion of power which brought us here, and caused our pulses to beat, and our affections to glow, and our minds to enter on the wonderful train of their operations. But if we consider the subject with a proper degree of attention, we shall be struck with amazement at the power which gave us life, and which is the origin of all our own powers. What power can compare with this of creation? What might is there, but that of God, which can set in motion the living economy of one human being? And here we are, my friends, in the midst of millions and millions of brethren, who have all received life from the same almighty and ever-quickening source, standing in our place among the generations which have been flowing down from the first human family, and are flowing on into the depths of uncertain time. What an exhibition of power is this vast sum of life, existing, as it does, independently of those who live; offered to us, forced upon us, to say so reverently, without an exertion or volition of our own.

If the beginning, the gift, the original impulse of life, is the expression of divine power, so is its continuance. How are we urged forward, through the several stages of our being, on to its final goal! The body grows, and the mind grows, to a certain point, and then we stop, and then we wear out and decay, — and all this by no effort or participation of our own; for who can add a cubit to his stature, or who can take one away? We rise up the hill, and the mightiest among us cannot accelerate his ascent; and then we turn and descend into the vale, and the mightiest among us cannot retard his going down. A conqueror may, if God permit him, overrun kingdoms and destroy cities, or build them up, and he may compel his fellow-men to lay their heads in humble vassalage upon his footstool, but yet he cannot keep himself from growing old. We are very proud sometimes; and we talk boastfully of what we have done and what we intend to do; but when gray hairs are scattered over our foreheads, we cannot bring the youthful color to their roots again; and when the mists of age begin to fall over the delicate orbs of sight, we find that with all our strength we cannot brush those little mists away. Forward and upward, and still forward, but downward, we are borne along, and we should strive as fruitlessly to resist the hand which impels us as to check the flowing or hinder the ebbing tides.

Also in the events of our lives, as well as in their continuance, we acknowledge a power in operation which is far greater than our own, and which can only belong to the Supreme Disposer. Liberty we have, indeed, and power we are intrusted with, but we cannot fail to perceive that our liberty and our power have their limits, beyond which they are not suffered to go. Else why are we so often disappointed in our expectations, and defeated in our designs, and overthrown in our enterprises; and why is that which is done against our intentions and efforts so often better for us than that would have been which we intended and strove to do? Where are the hopes which we had been carefully building up for the habitation of future years? Has not the wind of the Lord come and blown them away? And are not dwellings often provided for us, of firmer materials and a more excellent beauty, to the erection of which we have contributed neither labor nor thought? We cannot help feeling that we are free; but as little can we help feeling that our freedom is frequently bounded and controlled and directed by one whose right it is to rule. Nor can we resist the acknowledgment that the power which we most justly call our own is, at its origin, derived; and that we can do nothing which the Almighty does not enable us to do, either by immediate help, or by the original endowment of our ability. We shall be disposed, in fine, to confess and adore the presence of divine power in all that befalls us; in the beginning and continuance of life, in strength and weakness, in growth and decay, in circumstances prosperous or adverse, in rejoicing and mourning, in what is given and what is denied and what is taken away, in what we are permitted and assisted to do and what we are held from doing. In every condition, and under every posture of affairs, we shall perceive the same unvarying superintendence, and be ready to say with the Psalmist, "God hath spoken once; twice have I heard this; that power belongeth unto God."

II. In yet another way connected with our own being, do we hear the declaration of the text. We hear it in the mysterious accents of life; we hear it, too, in the no less mysterious, and to many the very fearful event of death. Here again is power; the power which suspends the motions which it caused, which dissolves the complicated workmanship which it organized, which chills the warm functions of vitality, and says to its creatures whom it formed of the dust, "Return, ye children of men!" We are not apt to be much impressed with the majesty of death, because it is of such common occurrence; but the truth is that dissolution is as wonderful as creation. We call it natural, because it constantly takes place; but the power which seals up the avenues of sense, sends away the speech, the feeling, and the thoughts from their accustomed tenement, and crushes up a breathing, firm, erect, proportioned frame into a few grains of fine dust, is a mighty power, a power which can only belong unto God. How certain, how irresistible is this power! Men are continually striving to elude it and protract their term of life, but they strive in vain; and, as if to prove to them that life is never in their own hands for a moment, the power of death comes upon them at every moment, from the period of birth on to the undefined boundary of extreme old age. How universal is this power! Generation after generation occupies the world, and then is swept away. A few names, a few deeds, a few monuments remain in each, and come down to its successors like dreams of a past night, and all the rest, together with every breath of life, are clean swept away. If it was not for the divine power of life, which more than supplies the vacancies occasioned by the divine power of death, how silent the earth would be in a little while! One by one we should lie down and be still, and the sounds of humanity would grow more and more faint, till at last they would be all hushed, and nothing would disturb the silence but the sighing of the winds, and the whispering of the trees, and the moans of the solitary sea. Is not here the impression of power? And should it be less, because such power is accompanied by a power of creation and animation, which keeps the world full and active, and resounding with the articulate voices of men? Truly the power of death is great and awful, and it belongs only unto God.

III. And terrible and oppressive would the thought of that power be, if we were not assured, both by the character of the Almighty, and his revealed word in the Gospel of Christ, that, as easily and as surely as he exercises the power of life and death, so easily and so surely will he put forth the power of reanimation. "Why should it be thought a thing incredible with you," said Paul to Agrippa, "that God should raise the dead?" It is not incredible at all, that he who causes us to live and causes us to die should also cause us to live again. The power of restoring life is not even wonderful when compared with the power of giving it, and the power of taking it away, and the other exertions of the power of God. But as they are wonderful, so also is this; and it appears to us more wonderful because it is not, like those others, the subject of our experience. And those others are the subjects of our experience only as we see them and are affected by them, and not as if we knew their essence or were acquainted with their modes of interior operation. If we will abstract ourselves for a while from the passing scene; if

we will cause our minds to stand apart from
the crowd of things in which they familiarly
and habitually move, so that, instead of being
borne along with them unthinkingly, they may,
as spectators, look regardfully upon them, and
seriously contemplate them; — and if we will
cease for a while to talk of nature, and reflect
on the agencies and existences which are about
us as really the work of nature's God, — then
the combinations and changes of the atmosphere, light, heat, motion, the wing of an insect, the leaf of a plant, — everything will
seem to us, and truly, to demand divine power,
and envelop a divine mystery, as well as does
the immortality of the soul. But the immortality of the soul, the future life, is a subject
which concerns us more deeply than any other
can, and is a subject which is removed from
the cognizance of our senses and our common
and daily habits; and therefore it especially
awes and excites the mind which is brought
into communion with it. That it does awe and
excite the mind is, however, no proof that
it is more wonderful in itself than many of
those things concerning which we never wonder, except when we think upon them intently.

Proof of man's immortality is to be sought
for in considerations of the character of God,
the nature of man, the promises and facts of

the gospel, and the evidences of that gospel's truth. In these we are to seek assurances — and if we seek in a right spirit we shall find them — that God *will* exercise the power of reanimating or continuing the life of the human soul. That he *can* exercise it, that it is not for his hand an extraordinary power, seems to be unquestionable; for he who can direct the least of those agencies which we see about us, can prevent the human soul from sharing in the death of the body, or confer life, with all its attributes, on the smallest particles of a former organization.

Once, twice, have we heard the solemn asseveration, that power belongeth unto God. There are also other words succeeding, which are full of encouragement, motive, and consolation. "And also unto thee, O Lord, belongeth mercy, for thou renderest unto every man according to his work." Infinite power and infinite mercy are lodged in the same hands, never to be divided, never to be alienated. O then that we may so order our works and ways before him that we may render ourselves fit objects of his mercy, and feel hope and confidence, instead of fear, when we contemplate his power; — that same hope and confidence which inspired the breast of the apostle, when he said, "I am persuaded that neither death nor life, nor angels, nor principalities, nor powers, nor things present, nor things to come, will ever be able to separate me from the love of God, which is in Christ Jesus our Lord."

OCTOBER 25, 1920.

SERMON IV.

GOD THE GUARDIAN OF SOULS.

Behold, all souls are mine. — *Ezek.* xviii. 4.

The Supreme Spirit speaks of the spirits which he has created. The Maker declares himself concerning the intelligent beings whom he has made. He claims his right in them, and over them, as his own. He is anxious to gain their attention to this claim; not that it can be resisted, but because it is full of the most solemn conclusions, and he would have it felt and pondered, and not neglected. Therefore he calls to us, that our ears may be opened and our hearts awakened. He says, "Behold!"— "Behold!" says the Almighty Father to his children, "all souls are mine."

This voice of God in revelation is not the only one by which his claim to our souls is preferred. Our own convictions, when we contemplate the vast and momentous subject, confirm in deep solemnity the revealed word, and show to us with irresistible proof, that we belong not to ourselves, but to one who made us, and who alone searches and knows us. The sense of our own weakness, the sense of our own ignorance, has each a voice which tells us of an ownership above us. And consciousness, which makes known to us the power and liberty which we have, marks out to us the bounds within which that power and liberty are confined, and intimates to us, by some of the most striking signs of our being and condition, how entirely dependent we are on a will which we cannot control, and on designs and determinations which we cannot fathom.

Let any one turn his thoughts inward, and think of that mysterious essence within him which thinks; let him meditate upon the soul which he calls his own; and let him say *how far* it is his own. It is his own in some respects, but in no respect which implies supreme and absolute possession. It is his own to vindicate against the undue influence and authority of all human beings and all earthly things. It is his own to keep from defilement; to guard from the entrance of sin; to cultivate and improve by the use of privileges and the application of circumstances; to bring into a willing subjection to the Father of spirits, conformity with his purposes, and imitation of his perfections; to prepare, through the mercy and help of God, for its happy reception into the heavenly world which is promised. In these respects, and they are important ones, his soul belongs to himself. But these imply no independent authority, no self-derived and original dominion. They imply a trust only, to be fulfilled or neglected, to be used or abused. The power and the liberty go no further. The soul of that man is his own in trust. He holds, that is to say, himself in trust, and by no power of his own. He feels that his whole being is dependent on some other being, which being can only be the Self-Existent. He feels that the possession of himself is not in himself; that he is not his own, but God's.

He communes with himself thus: What am I? What is this thinking, sentient, active principle or being which is my soul — myself? What is its nature? What its composition? How was it made? How did it begin to be? I know that I am. I am conscious that my soul lives. But what is my soul, and how does it live? This I know not, and am conscious that I cannot know. It seems to me as if my soul existed in some dark and impenetrable depth, showing itself faintly, as it were, by a few outward signs upon the surface of its dwelling-place, but deeper than this wrapt up from even its own searchings. I am not insignificant. I can call up the past. I can interrogate the future. I can visit infinite heights and depths. I can long for glory and joy which are unknown and afar. My soul is a wondrous existence, and worthy to be known, and must be known; — but I know it not; it knows not itself. How can I be the absolute owner of that which I do not know? The creating and eternal Intellect knows me and owns me. My soul is his. All souls are his.

And I am confident, such an one may say, that this my ignorance, which happily places me in the hands of the All-wise, is not an ignorance peculiar to myself. I am confident that it is common to all men. Let the doubter doubt as much, and the freethinker think as freely, or, what is often the same thing with him, as licentiously as he will, yet their ignorance of the manner of their own being is a truth which they cannot deny. Neither can they deny that they are, and that they think. Consciousness obliges them to confess that they have souls; but with all their pretended wisdom, they cannot explain what their souls are, nor assume the actual possession of them to themselves. They may talk as they please, but they must feel sometimes in the power of One who made them and owns them, who knows them and judges them. Their ignorance cannot always make them bold and Heaven-defying. It must sometimes lead them, as mine leads me, to the feet of Him who knows us, and to whom therefore we must belong.

This soul of mine! I cannot express my sense of the mysteriousness which envelops it, and the entire dependence in which it hangs every moment on its Creator. Is it of its essence and mode of being only that I am ignorant? What do I know of its course, its path, the changes of its condition, the varieties of its lot? Do I know with any precision what motives will be presented to it at any future season? Do I know what trials await it? what joys or what sorrows are in store for it? what voices will speak to it? Can I anoint its eyes, so that it shall be able to behold one secret of coming time? Can I tell when it will be summoned to part from the body? Have I the least power over its very existence? Were the sentence of dread annihilation to be issued against it, could I do the least thing to arrest that sentence? Could I say, It shall not die? Or have I the power of annihilation over it, so that I can say, It shall not live? Who is so vain, so mad, as to assert that he possesses either these powers? How absolutely we belong to God!

This soul of mine! The more I think of it, the less seems to be my authority over it. A large portion of its existence while here on earth is passed in that inscrutable state of sleep; or, if it be denied that the soul ever sleeps, in that state, still inscrutable, which it occupies while the body sleeps. My body must sleep. Life would depart from it, if it did not sleep. Its powers must be refreshed by slumber, and so, while the mind continues its companion, must the powers of the mind be so refreshed. I cannot therefore prevent the change which passes over the soul, and remains upon it periodically, and for a large portion of my mortal life. And while my body is sleeping, where is my soul, and what power have I over it? Perhaps it wanders back to the days of my childhood, and converses face to face with those from whom I am divided by half the world's circumference, or by the grave. And then suddenly it will be on the tops of mountains, or in pathless forests, or in vaulted and interminable caves, or in strange, twilight, indescribable scenes, holding disjointed and unintelligible language with itself, or with shadowy beings for whom there is no name. But wherever it is, or whatever it is doing, as soon as I awake it returns to me, and is restored from its change, — a change incomprehensible to me, to itself. I hold no clue to its goings. I often understand not where it has been, and endeavor in vain to unravel the ideas which have occupied it; and often I am unable to tell whether it has or has not been active during this interval of sleep. Memory presents me with no object on its mirror. Consciousness is silent. How entirely am I out of my own power in sleep. Who holds me during those misty hours? Watchman of Israel! who never slumberest nor sleepest, thou compassest my path and my lying down; thou art the guardian of my soul while my tired head is on the pillow, and my judgment, like an over-wearied sentinel, is drooping unconsciously at its post; thou knowest the way that I take when I know it not myself, and when I awake I am still with thee! How can a man, who will reflect a moment on these perpetually recurring periods of sleep, fail to be struck and affected by the view of the helplessness of his soul in those periods, its need of protection, the kindness and constancy which are necessary to its protection? How can a man think of sleep, without being impressed seriously and religiously? without feeling that his soul is God's?

This soul of mine! or which I call mine, and yet is mine so imperfectly! it now performs its functions regularly and connectedly. In my waking hours, and when its sight is undimmed by passion or by sin, it perceives objects clearly, or with such clearness as this earthly atmosphere allows ; it exercises its reasoning powers, such as they may be, with order and distinctness ; it holds an acknowledged intercourse with other souls. But how long will it certainly maintain this sound estate? I may guard it, it is my given duty to guard it, against some of the causes of derangement, which I may ward off by vigilance, by temperance, by self-discipline ; but how can I guard it against many other causes, visible and invisible, which may come upon it unawares, and destroy its balance, and confuse its operations, and strike its whole fabric into tangled disarrangement? A wound in the body, or in itself; a blow on the head, or a sorrow in the heart; a violent fever ; a gradual and insurmountable declension ; or some influence altogether unknown and unsearchable, may surprise this soul of mine, and cut it off from rational communication with mankind. I may pray that its sanity may be preserved amid all these dangers ; but I cannot assure myself that it will be. I can enter into no engagement with my soul, to secure it against them. I should only mock it were I to do so. The condition from which it shrinks may be its own, as it has been that of other men. And should it be, who will hold it, keep it, sustain it, when the little authority that I ever had over it is taken away? How dark seems the darkness! how sad the wandering of mental derangement! And yet there is a ray of light amidst the deepest gloom, and the sound of a comforting voice in the most intricate windings of the labyrinth. The ray streams down from heaven, and the voice is that which declares, "All souls are mine!" All souls are in the hand of their Keeper and Defender. Not one is excepted. God preserves the roaming, irresponsible soul through all its aberrations, and, notwithstanding the outward signs of loss, saves all its faculties, and permits not a fraction of its integrity to be dissolved. Of this truth he often affords us the most convincing proofs. Often does the soul, which has been untuned for years, utter in the last moments of mortality the clear notes of restoration and praise. Often does the soul, which, for a melancholy time has seemed to be shattered, broken down, and undone, rise up just as it is called to quit the infirm body, rise up in the wholeness and freshness of former days, show how safely it has been led and held by the almighty arm, and then resign itself to its God. So manifestly does the Father of spirits vindicate the truth of his declaration, "All souls are mine." They cannot stray from under his eye; they cannot be lost from his care.

You will perceive that what I have said of the soul's ignorance of itself, and weakness in and by itself, clashes not at all with what may be urged concerning its high powers, and the intimations which it gives of higher destinies. The views of its infirmity on the one hand, and of its dignity on the other, are religious views, pointing to the same great result. Its hopes, its longings, its workings, its capacity of improvement, its generous affections, these show that it is, and that it is worthy to be cared for; while the want of all knowledge of its essential self, the changes which come over it in spite of itself, its wanderings, as it were, away from itself, all show the necessity of its being cared for by some one who is greater than itself. My main design has been to prove that the wants of the soul direct it to a Maker and Preserver. I have presented one illustration of the old position, "I am, and therefore God must be." Not that God's existence is dependent on ours, — God forbid the vain imagination, — but that our existence is dependent on his, and denotes his as that on which it must depend. In this manner is exposed the fallacy of those who pretend to say, that because they are ignorant of the soul's essence therefore it does not exist. The answer is, that consciousness attests its existence, and its very ignorance of its own essence attests its God. I know not myself, — and therefore there must be One who knows me. I cannot sustain myself, — and therefore there must be One who sustains me. Give your thoughts intently, my friends, at any time to this subject, and you will feel, with an energy to which words can do no justice, that you are depending, resting, every instant, upon your Maker, your God.

"Behold!" says the Eternal, "all souls are mine." "Yea!" respond our souls, from the deep places of their ignorance, and with all the voices of their wants, — "Yea! all souls are thine!" Thou art their Father, Owner, Keeper. The souls of the lofty and the lowly, of the wealthy and the poor, of the happy and the sorrowful, — all souls are thine. In the feebleness of childhood and the feebleness of age; in clouds and darkness and weariness; from the first moment of their existence to the last of their sojourn in clay; in their searchings after thee and departures from thee, and whether they know thee or know thee not, all souls are thine! Take them — they are surrendered to thee! Help their weakness, heal their sickness, enlighten their blindness. Keep them in the knowledge and love of thee and of thy Son. Let them live in thy countenance, and grow in thy grace, and find thy redeeming mercy. And raise them at last, O, our God, from these poor houses to those heavenly courts, where they shall know and love thee more, and serve and enjoy thee forever!

December 6, 1835.

SERMON V.

FOLLY OF ATHEISM.

The fool hath said in his heart, There is no God. — *Psalm* xiv. 1.

These same words commence also the fifty-third Psalm, which is almost an exact repetition of the fourteenth. They express the sentiment as strongly as possible, that to deny the being of God is a demonstration of the want of wisdom, of the abuse of intellect, of exceeding folly. They find an echo, commonly, in our own bosoms. Having received the idea of a God of infinite perfection, and having cherished it into faith, and being deeply convinced of its unspeakable value, we are amazed at the rejection of it by any, and at once decide that such a rejection is incompatible with soundness of mind. To us it is an idea, a conviction, a faith, so full of majesty, of love, of hope, of power, and protection, so preëminently the light of our mental and moral being, that we would lose anything, suffer anything, rather than part with it; and are unable to believe that they who renounce it and contend against it are in possession of even a tolerably well-guided understanding.

It is probably this feeling of the folly of atheistic views which sometimes renders us a little impatient of those discourses which aim to prove the existence of God, in refutation of atheism, especially if it be by a metaphysical train of argument. We say to ourselves that we do not need the refutation; that we do not wish to have the existence of God proved to us. We fear that some deficiency of matter or manner, some feebleness of proof, some inaptitude of illustration, may do injustice to the high theme, and yield advantage to the adversary; or, if we entertain not this fear, we are simply unwilling to hear a truth regularly demonstrated, of which we have already the fullest conviction, and which we deem it the extreme of foolishness or wickedness to deny. It seems to be lingering too long in the elements.

It is not to be doubted that this repugnance may itself become too sensitive, and be carried too far. We should be tolerant of the repetition of arguments which may be interesting and instructive to others, if not to us, and from which we ourselves, in some former time, may have derived no small share of the present strength of our convictions. Though we do not absolutely need proof of the being of God, yet it may be useful to dwell upon the steps of it presented to us; and though nothing quite new may be advanced in the way of argument, yet something may be said which shall either awaken a slumbering memory, or point out a new track for our thoughts, in the way of suggestion. Neither is it always the purpose of a discourse on the being of God to prove that being to those who may be in doubt of it, but, quite as often or oftener, to conduct the meditations of the faithful over some portion of a subject which covers an almost inexhaustible field of inquiry and reflection, and everywhere contains material of pious and profitable thought.

But though caution is to be had in regulating the repugnance of which I have spoken, it remains true that it arises from a sound conviction of the folly of unbelief, and deserves notice as an indication of its pure and healthy source. What indeed can be more senseless — and this is the point to which I would now direct your attention — than the act of denying the existence of a Supreme Being, of discarding the thought of an Almighty Creator, Disposer, and Friend? What good end can there be proposed by it; what satisfaction; what reward? What is there to be gained, and what is there not to be lost, by the prodigal renunciation of faith in God? This is one of the most simple and practical views of the whole subject. In a moral aspect, it is the test-question. It reaches the end. It touches the moral and spiritual influences of religious faith.

What in effect is the atheistic declaration? He who says that there is no God, says, in the first place, not only that there is no creator, who with knowledge and design brought into existence and set in motion the whole scene of things about us, but that there is no mind which thoroughly understands and comprehends this universe, and penetrates its many mysteries, and takes it into an omniscient charge. If there is no knowledge of it, there can be no charge of it. The world is uncared for. It is without a ruler, without a protector. Is there any wisdom in a supposition like this? Is there anything pleasant or satisfactory to the mind or heart to be told that the world goes on by itself, and may stop and fall to pieces of itself; that there is no one that understands its numberless operations, above and beneath, which produce such magnificent and beautiful results; that its mysteries always have been and always will be impenetrable; that it is without a governor and without a guide? Is not the assertion as far from wisdom as the east is from the west?

And then, if the world is unknown and uncared for, it follows of course that man is unknown and uncared for by a Supreme Being. He who says that there is no God, says that he himself, says that every man, is without government, without protection, without salvation, is in a condition of solitariness and orphanage. He says that there is no judge to right the wronged, to defend the cause of the needy and oppressed, to restore the golden balance of justice and truth which has been disturbed by passion and by crime. He says, that, when the spirit of a man is bowed down by calamity and is deserted by human sympathy, there is no one above to resort to for strength and for sympathy; that, when it is lingering on the last verge of life, there is no one to sustain and comfort it; and when it passes out of life, there is no one to receive it. He says that there is no one to give us what the world cannot give, but that all our peace and all our joy and all our reward must be here or nowhere, and that when happiness departs from us here, it departs from us forever. He says that the widow has no Eternal Friend, and the orphan no Almighty Father; that we are all orphans; that there is no paternal eye to watch over us, and no paternal hand to lead us, and no paternal heart to feel for us, and no paternal home to shelter us at last; that we live thus forlorn and die thus forlorn, proceeding from oblivion and returning to oblivion again. This is what he says, saying that there is no God. Is there any wisdom in the opinion; any mark of wisdom about it? Is there anything elevating, or comforting, or edifying in it? Is there anything in it conducive to virtue or to any kind of improvement? Is it not folly, and the height of folly, to divest one's self of convictions of a supreme order, and a providential guidance, and a parental and eternal love? Yet this is the folly of him who says that there is no God.

And he says this, be it further observed, not in obedience to a confessed preponderance of logical, or any other species of argument against the existence of God. No preponderance of the kind has ever been confessed. On the contrary, the preponderance is claimed by believers to be vastly on their own side. They rest not their cause on feeling alone, however confidently they rely upon feeling. They have store of argument beside; and can match, out of their armory, any weapon which the adversary can produce. No argument against the existence of God has ever been uttered into the reluctant world, which has not been immediately encountered by a stronger argument from the ranks of the faithful. For every discourse, every book, in favor of the atheistic hypothesis, there are scores of discourses, scores of books, in refutation of it, and all better. And this is so, whether we go into the fields of metaphysical speculation, or into the varied regions of natural science. There is a line, indeed, beyond which human investigation cannot proceed, beyond which it cannot be said, This is, or This is not. But up to this absolute line, where all must stop in a common ignorance, every argument of unbelief, from every quarter, has been met and answered, ably, fairly, and completely. He, therefore, who says there is no God, makes the assertion not only in defiance of the most prevailing moral considerations, but in neglect, also, of as powerful reasoning as ever proceeded from the combination of human genius with human learning. What unspeakable folly — to sacrifice hope, trust, protection, consolation, without being able to say that the greater array of reason, or that some unanswered argument compelled the sacrifice! What unspeakable folly — to reject the sure staff of support in this world of trouble, without the substitute of a single deduction of science which has not been proved unsound, or of a cold syllogism even, which has not been broken in pieces!

While we are upon this moral and practical

view of atheism, it may be well to add, that the folly which has been exposed is not in the least diminished by a denial of the term atheism, though at the same time a theory is adopted, which, however ingenious it may look as a theory, is morally and practically atheistic. If an existence or principle is supposed to pervade the world, or be the mind or soul of the world, and is invested with the name of God, but is yet divested of the personal and intelligent care and government of the world and all the creatures in it, then there is no difference whatever, in a moral and practical view, between this impersonal principle, called God, and no God. If the principle called God has no care of or for me, if my heart cannot call him God and Father, if there are no grounds in his existence for the exercise of my love, my fear, my hope, and my trust, then it is of no consequence to me whether such a principle exists or not. I will not even waste my time in ascertaining whether there is, metaphysically, any difference between a theory which supposes such a God and the baldest form of atheism, because I feel that, morally and practically and vitally, there is no difference. Indeed it may be easily asserted, and it will be as easily granted, that no one can form a distinct conception of the mode of God's existence; can with any accuracy define the Infinite Lord of heaven and earth. But this inability does not interfere with the power of forming a moral apprehension of God, which is, in fact, the basis of all true religion. It is not necessary that we should be able to define the mode of God's existence, but it is necessary, and it is perfectly within our power, to make up our minds whether the God of our faith is or is not a God, who, amidst all the mysteries of his nature, has a personal knowledge and a personal charge of us; whether he is the God of the Bible and of Christianity, or of some metaphysical theory which would remove him from the government of the world and the affections of men. It is very easy for any one to settle for himself this moral and practical question, which is without a shadow of abstruseness. He has to deal only with results, with consequences. He has only to determine whether there is any final distinction, any distinction which his heart can recognize, between a God who sees and knows and hears and loves him not, and no God. If he perceives no such distinction, he will not feel more inclined to surrender his long-cherished faith and worship to an adorned theory, hung about with lofty phrases, than to a more vulgar atheism; and he would consider the surrender to be a folly of the same character, and to the same effect, with that of saying, There is no God.

"The fool hath said in his heart, There is no God." His folly consists not in his saying so, merely; not in the use of that single phrase; it is not a folly of speech only; it is the folly of his heart, by which he banishes from his thoughts, as far as he can, the conviction of an overruling, all-seeing, rewarding, and faithful God. All speculation which results in a similar conclusion must be marked by a similar epithet. The true God is ascertained, not speculatively, but morally. He is God the Creator, God the Father, God the Judge. As a human friend sees us and knows us, so does God, only far more clearly and intimately; as that friend feels for us and loves us, so does God, only far more deeply and more wisely; as that friend seeks our happiness for time and for eternity, so does God, but by means which are far beyond all human power or thought. Faith in this God is the true faith, be it accompanied or unaccompanied by speculation; it is wisdom, and it is salvation. "For this God is our God forever and ever; he will be our guide even unto death."

OCTOBER 17, 1841.

SERMON VI.

DWELLING IN THE TEMPLE.

One thing have I desired of the Lord, that will I seek after; that I may dwell in the house of the Lord all the days of my life, to behold the beauty of the Lord, and to inquire in His temple. — *Psalm* xxvii. 4.

The existence and perfections of God, and the relations of God with man, as his Creator, Father, and Judge, being established as facts in the mind of the believer, the very next question which will naturally be presented for solution is, what should be his own main object and chief desire, as a creature, a son, and a servant of God? The question is, not what should be his only object and desire, but what should be his principal, his supreme object and desire. He sees and readily allows, that while he is on earth, surrounded by various earthly relations, his objects must be many and his desires many, and that it is the law of his condition and the will of his Creator that he should give due heed to them all, in their time and place. But he requires to know, beside and above this, what should be the ruling desire of his spirit, which should hold a supervision over the others, and according to which the others should be conformed, and which will serve him as a great guiding principle through the labyrinth of life.

Many of us, I presume, at one period or another, and with more or less intensity, have considered this same question. Remarkable and pitiable is the lethargy or frivolity of that soul to which it has never been brought home. But sickness, or bereavement, or solitude, any signal interruption of or departure from our usual routine of living, or even the seemingly casual intervention of some serious train of thought, is apt to propose, and lead us on to answer the question, what, among all our desires, should be the chief desire; what, as rational and immortal beings, we should be living for? And all argument, all reflection, all self-communion, soberly and sensibly conducted, will soon be concentrated on one point, toward which all other circumstances will look, and on which all the energies of the mind, and occupations and engagements of life will be made eventually to bear. The reason and heart will unite in the conclusion, that the chief desire of the creature should be to remember and serve his Creator; of the child, to honor and obey his Father; of the mortal probationer, to obtain the favor of his Judge. This conclusion is well expressed by the words of the text: "One thing have I desired of the Lord, that will I seek after; that I may dwell in the house of the Lord all the days of my life, to behold the beauty of the Lord, and to inquire in," or, as it is otherwise translated, "to gaze upon his temple."

The one great object and purpose of rational and spiritual life is expressed by these words none the less distinctly, and all the more impressively, by being expressed somewhat metaphorically. The one desire of the Psalmist was, that he might dwell in the house of the Lord all the days of his life. But the Psalmist, with all his attachment, as a Jew, to the temple at Jerusalem, did not mean that the one thing on which his heart was bent was actually to take up his abode, and literally to dwell and remain in the temple all the days of his life; but habitually, constantly, and gladly to frequent it, as a devout worshipper, and in order that his heart might be prevailingly occupied and refreshed by the true spirit and the gracious comforts of religion. As it was to him, so this constant spiritual abiding in the house of the Lord will appear to be to us, in our seasons of reflection and inquiry, the one thing to be desired and sought after. Not that the mere going to the house of God is this "one thing," or the mere staying there, ever so long or often; but that the sense of dependence on God, the emotions of gratitude towards him, and the giving up ourselves to him in love and obedience, which are figured by the strong expression of dwelling always in the house of the Lord, will be to us the "one thing," to which the desires of the heart should be turned, and into which our life should be absorbed. The purpose of the soul will be simple. It will no longer be distracted by many calls, bewildered among many roamings; it will be directed to one thing, even the perpetual worship of the Father in spirit and in truth. This worship is not words alone, or words chiefly, or any outward forms. Words and outward forms may and do nourish it, furnishing it with signs and memorials; and therefore it will not hastily, and it cannot safely, refuse their aid; but the worship itself is real service, the service which the affections, the actions, the whole and complete life, render to the One Supreme. And whether we say the love of God, or the fear of God, or religion, or piety, or holiness, or the obedience of God's commandments, it is all the same; it is "one thing," and *the* one thing which attracts the chief desire of the creature when he feels himself to be the creature of God. On this one thing is fixed intently the heart of the true worshipper, the heart which has been fixed thereon by his own rational convictions, and the divine grace assisting him. The house of God, built with hands, will be loved and frequented, because it is the visible type of the temple not built with hands, and because it is the porch of the temple within. But the temple of his soul's constant residence, the house of the Lord, in which he desires to dwell his whole life long, is that lofty and spiritual building, that vast and sacred edifice, higher than the sky and more ample than the earth, which encloses all his relations with the Author of his being. In this he serves and ministers, a faithful Levite, by night and by day, feeding the bright and perpetual lamp of faith, singing the psalms of the heart, and offering the sacrifices of God in righteousness. He is not wearied with his service. He feels no impatience, and no morbid desire of change. He is not to be attracted nor terrified from the place of his duty; for he has found the place of his duty to be the place, and the only place, of his security and rest. In suffering or rejoicing, in action or repose, in the body or out of the body, he desires one thing above everything else, — to dwell in the house of the Lord, to be with God.

This desire is rendered more single and intense, more searching and sustaining, pervading the soul as the red blood the body, by the varied events of life. True it is that many who, in some rare and thoughtful season, have entertained it, afterwards dismiss it, or let it faint away, and that many either do not form it at all, or only breathe it hastily with their last breath, when it is probably too late, at least for all purposes of this mortal probation. But I speak of those who do form it, and who are daily receiving from experience some useful lessons, here a little and there a little, of seriousness and wisdom. They will acknowledge that their discipline is never too much, and always fraught with benefit, if the spirit will apply it wisely; and that every year which passes over them, whatever its character may be, still confirms the conviction that one thing is to be desired and sought after, which is, to dwell forever in the house of the Lord.

Though every year and all events confirm this conviction, and concur to strengthen the chief desire of the conscious and watchful spirit, yet there are peculiar seasons and occasions in which clearer views than usual seem to be obtained of the great object of life, and a stronger impulse than common to be given to the supreme desire. I have already intimated what some of these seasons and occasions are. The soul is then compelled or kindly led into a state of separation. We enter into our chambers. Worldly forms, gay temptations, the shapes of fashion and of custom, are then shut out. The eye reposes from their flauntings, and the ear is relieved from their babblings; and in their stead comes in duty, and sits down by us alone, and utters its simple but solemn lessons, and teaches us in serious friendliness the purposes of our existence. The listener, the pupil, is brought to a survey of the years that are past. He sees them in a clear and passionless light; and the conviction comes to him like a revelation; it is so unlike what he has at other times called convictions, that in measure they have been brief, in number few; and that all their value, all that renders them of more consequence than so many successive dreams, is comprised in acts of obedience to the supreme law, in works and thoughts of charity, in the exercise of the affections according to the divine will, in whatever has brought him nearer, by the ways of action or contemplation, to heaven, Christ, and God. What are commonly termed the pleasures of life, shrink up in this survey into a small compass, and are so little inviting in their shrunken forms, that the mind would rather avoid them than dwell upon them. Those only seem to be pleasures which have been received with gratitude and enjoyed with innocence, and have united themselves with duties in the great work of spiritual preparation. Nor does the pupil look only on the years that are past. His view is directed to the future. He looks down on the valley before him, where falls the broad, shadowless light of eternity. Years and months are not there, for they have not yet come. But the signs of his destiny are plain. He reads, that if his mortal life be near its close, the untried state is also near, and God, the Judge, is at hand. He reads, that if his life is to be spared for more years on earth, they will be no longer than the years that are gone, and will pass as swiftly as they did; and that, whatever their number or character may be, their value will surely be measured by the same unvarying rule which tested the value of their predecessors, and that thoughts and deeds of holiness and improvement will be the only records upon them which he will peruse hereafter with any satisfaction. He sees that his fortunes may change, but that his great obligations cannot; and that, whatever else may be altered, his relations with the Eternal Father must remain unalterable. And thus he feels himself even now encompassed before and behind, on the right hand and on the left, by the presence of that unchangeable One. His contemplations are rendered distinct, simple, and satisfactory. He no longer labors among things which are hard to be understood. He learns the few letters which compose the ineffable Name. Life, and the presence of its author are to him one and the same thing, and the ends of life become identified with the obedience and the enjoyment of God.

Convictions of this character are the only ones which deserve the name of being religious. Other convictions there may be, or seem to be, enthusiastic, sympathetic, traditionary, or doctrinal, which claim to be religious; but unless they guide the affections, the desires, the life, into the state of spiritual obedience, trust and rest which I have attempted to describe, they are not religious, they are not Christian; they are nothing, and vanity. Their pretensions, however great, cannot be allowed. They will not be heard for their much speaking. Those convictions only are religious which are active and operative, leading the soul into the temple, and causing it to dwell there. By whatever circumstances, events, instructions, or trains of thought such convictions are produced, they are essentially religious. They may be brought about in one mind by one set of influences, and in another mind by a set in many respects dissimilar; but, however brought about, the mind which entertains them entertains religion, finds religion, enjoys religion;— and enjoyment it is, above all else which bears the name.

And here it may not be unnecessary to say, that these proper religious convictions are far from being of a gloomy nature. They neither cause gloominess, nor have they any affinity with such a temperament. On the contrary, the more firmly they are settled in the mind of the worshipper, the more constant and undisturbed will be his cheerfulness, — that rational cheerfulness which is the inseparable companion of rational seriousness. His most serious thoughts are employed in laying the foundations of cheerfulness, so that no light shock shall overturn it. Cheerfulness becomes part of his character, part of his nature. How should he be otherwise than cheerful, when he feels that his spirit abides with the Paternal Spirit under the paternal dome? How should he be otherwise than cheerful, when he feels that under that dome there is peace and security forever, that into that sanctuary the enemy and the avenger cannot pursue him? How should he be otherwise than cheerful, when he regards appointed sorrows as means of improvement and happiness, and finds in practice that they are so indeed; when he sees that flowers spring up from graves; when he sees that grief penetrates and enriches the willing soul as does the rain the willing soil; when he sees that death cannot harm his life, nor change his substantial relations with its eternal Giver and Preserver? I will not say that he is at every moment cheerful; that he is not sometimes overtaken by the shadow of dark hours. He is not stoically independent of all outward impressions, nor exempt from internal changes. He is not perfect. He is mortal. He is frail. But his cheerfulness, though not actually unintermitted, is yet habitual. It does not easily give way. It is more and more confirmed by the accession of every feeling of piety, every religious experience, every step towards the innermost, holiest, and safest portion of the house of the Lord.

Thus are they instructed who are willing to receive instruction. Thus are they instructed day by day, and day by day improved. Their outward occupations, their temporal business and pursuits, and the scenes of them, are various. Whatever these may be, they will not slight them. They will move in them with diligence. But they will perceive, all the while, that, being temporal, they can only endure for a season, and cannot wisely be made the sole and ultimate object of attention and desire; and that there is only *one thing*, amidst all these vanishing things, which is supremely desirable, — to dwell in the house of the Lord; to obey him, to worship him, to rest upon him forever; because he, and he only, is the master of life, and without him favor is deceitful and beauty is vain, light is darkness and life is death.

FEBRUARY 22, 1835.

SERMON VII.

DEATH AN APPOINTMENT.

It is appointed unto men once to die, but after this the judgment. — *Heb.* ix. 27.

We cannot think or speak of death except as a certainty. It would amount even to a misuse of language to say, We *may* die, as if the event were in any degree conditional, instead of employing the positive and only proper phrase, We *must* die. There is a wide difference, however, between regarding death merely as a *fact*, though settled and inevitable, and regarding it as an *appointment*. To regard it merely as a fact, universal to the human race, is to give it into the cold hands of an unintelligent fate. To regard it as an appointment, is to place it under the direction of an intelligent cause or being. And this last is the conclusion to which we most naturally are led. Nothing seems to be more unreasonable than to attribute death, which has its prescribed laws and limits, to the action of lawless chance or insensible fate. Its laws are ascertained by the science of physiology; its limits are well known to general experience. The sure elements of death are contained, from the first, within the structure of every human frame, premonishing its dissolution; and this dissolution takes place within certain bounds of time, which are never exceeded. Here are indications of intention; signals that death does not happen unto, but is appointed unto men.

Then the question occurs, If death is appointed, by whom is it appointed? By Him only, is the necessary answer, — the One Almighty, who appoints all the conditions of our being and of the world, and who alone is able to appoint a condition so dread and so universal as that of death. By none other can death be appointed. By none other can generation after generation be swept away from the earth, like leaves by autumnal winds. Death is an appointment from God.

Here we arrive at the religious view of death, having passed the merely literal and the merely philosophical view. Here we ascribe a significance to death, and a holy significance, by making it the act of God. Here we perceive that the proper meaning and force of the text lies in the word "appointed." The idea of God's supreme power and providence must have occupied the mind of the writer, or he would not have written, " It is appointed unto men once to die." And it is in this view of death only, as a divine appointment, that comfort is to be found when the shadow of death is passing over us. For if God has taken this event into his immediate charge, if death be of his appointing, then we may certainly know that, whatever may be the terrors of its appearance, it is appointed in wisdom and appointed in love. It is appointed by the same Being who opens our eyes upon the glories of this marvellous world, and is the author of all the happiness we have ever enjoyed. It is appointed by the same Being who rules the universe, in all its movements and throughout all its extent. Let it come, then, at whatever season, in whatever mode, it cannot come without the cognizance of that knowledge which precludes the supposition of error, and of that mercy on which every doubt and every sorrow may lean. The circumstances of death may indeed be varied by that imprudence which is a part of human frailty, or that perverseness which is a consequence of human liberty. But neither human ignorance nor sin can fatally interfere with the wisdom and love of God. The event of death is unalterably of his appointment, equally with his kindest and brightest dispensations, and being so, cannot be separated from those attendant comforts which flow from his grace, and are founded on his divine nature and attributes. Nor can any shock of the excited elements, or anything called fatal accident, disturb the settled pillars of this faith. All these are under his control, pass not a step beyond his decree, and touch not the great issue. The wildest waves sink down with the subsiding storm, and yield a path to following navies. The fiercest volcano retires, when spent, into its caverns, and leaves a soil for the richest vineyards on the highway of its desolations. Life follows death and death life, and both by the same appointment. To know that God is wise, to know that God is good, is to know that his wisdom and his goodness preside at once over life and over death.

We soon reach the conclusion that the event of death is a direct appointment of the Supreme Intelligence, and that it therefore admits freely of those comforts which a consideration of the attributes of our heavenly Father cannot fail to afford. But we are permitted to proceed somewhat further, and to ask more particularly why is death appointed, and what are the special grounds of the appointment? A complete answer to this question, satisfying every wish of the heart and every difficulty of the understanding, must not be expected in this present state, which is emphatically a state of dimness; but full enough may be answered for the encouragement of patience, of hope, and of unbounded trust.

All the arrangements of man's present life have an evident temporary character, and a reference to a speedy termination; manifesting the want of things not now attainable, and a series of preparations for some contemplated change. The body itself, the abode of the individual man, is not a structure built up for permanence. The very food by which it is nourished often becomes the means of its injury or destruction. The slightest attack shakes it. Invisible atoms in the air accomplish its decay. If it escapes all violence, all disease, it wears out of itself, according to the laws of its construction, and with no means of repair. Bounds are set to our knowledge and to our spiritual experience. The thousands of stars just show themselves to us, and only by night and in the least appreciable degree, and never draw any nearer, but remain as far away at our maturity as at our birth. Of life, and its principal conditions and essential relations, we soon learn all that there is to be learned. The details of knowledge are indeed inexhaustible and always enough for occupation, and are only too much neglected; but they are all contained within an earthly circle, and make no addition to those conditions and relations of which I speak. The man who numbers thirty or forty years of pilgrimage must feel that, with regard to these main objects, he has *got through*, and that the rest of his way can be only repetition. Our faculties themselves have their limits, beyond which there is no increase for them; just as the body, when arrived at its full strength, grows no stronger. Here are indications of sufficient distinctness to show that there is only so much to be done in this life, so much to be known, so much to be experienced, and no more. And yet, together with these indications, there is an irrepressible desire in the bosom of man, who is thus limited and hemmed in, for the further expansion and progress which the terms of his present being deny to him. Death is appointed to fulfil this desire, by removing the limits and restrictions which the initiatory state of existence imposes. To perceive the temporary nature and frailty and deficiency of mortal life, is to perceive a reason for the appointment of death.

Again, let us consider that the field of this life is full of the springs of sorrow, and that these springs, or a large proportion of them, have their origin in the conditions of its imperfection. The pains and sicknesses of the body, the infirmities and errors of the mind, the wanderings and excesses of the passions, are all the sources of many and great sorrows, and of sins which are sorrows also. But these sources of sorrow belong to the limited condition of life, and will stop when that condition ends. Their purpose is no doubt disciplinary and useful; but it is consoling to be assured that they will be brought to a close by the closing of that temporary arrangement from which they arise and to which they are bound. Death is appointed, then, to hush these sorrows in the act of terminating this arrangement; and it is appointed to act, not by extinction, but by change, — not by putting an end to being itself, and consequently all that belongs to it, but by putting an end to a limited state of being and all the troubles which are inseparable from its limitations.

But death itself, which is appointed to cut off the sources of many sorrows, is it not, in the execution of this office, the author of other and overwhelming sorrows? The sobs and tears of widows and orphans, and those of other name among the bereaved, answer without a word, and testify most forcibly that it is. The dear affections which grow out of the consanguinities and connections of domestic life must needs be wounded when those relations are broken by death. To love here on earth is indeed to prepare the way for sorrow; for all who love must be parted by the great appointment. But daeth is appointed to put an end also to this sorrow. It is appointed to put an end to that state which requires death. Its first, last, and only act is to open a scene of things in which its own power is forever abdicated. The text informs us that "it is appointed unto men once to die." We die that we may die no more. What a boundless scene is opened by that word "once." Years will roll on, and there will be no symptoms of old age or decay; centuries will elapse, and there will be no fear, no thought of dying; for they who have died once shall die no more, death having no place nor part in the dominion to which he has brought them. What a scene of enlargement and advancement is that in which there will be no decline of the faculties, no walls for their imprisonment, no chains binding them to the set rounds of mortality. What a scene of holiness, in which those causes of sin shall cease which now operate through the infirmities of the flesh. What a scene of happiness, in which those sources of sorrow must necessarily be dried up which now flow from sickness, from separation, from death. We die once and but once. Death was appointed that it might be lost in life.

This future and eternal life is also, in all its conditions, an appointment of the same Eternal Being who appoints the present life and death. Judgment is a condition of that life. "It is appointed unto men once to die, but after this the judgment." Death is done with, having fulfilled the purposes of its appointment, and the eternal life begins its course in judgment. What the place of each soul may be, as it enters this life without death, we may not know; but we know that the righteous God will judge the world in righteousness.

Let us learn to look on death as an appointment, not a fatality; as an appointment of our Heavenly Father, who alone has the power; as appointed in wisdom and love, because appointed by Him. To die is not to be lost, but to acquire a more certain and distinguished being. To die is to be set free — free from the fetters of a body which is dying while it lives, and from the narrow bounds of a restricted state. To die is to go with our conscience and character only into the presence of our Judge. To every temple there is a portal, and a passage from the one to the other. This mortal life is the portal which stands before the grand temple of eternity, and death is the passage between them.

September 12, 1841.

SERMON VIII.

THE TIME OF DEATH.

A time to die. — *Eccles.* iii. 2.

FEW and simple as these words are, they are full of meaning. Reflection will reveal to us something of this fulness. It is well for us if we be accustomed to reflect, and do not stand among those who only perceive, — who only see the surface, the outside, and there stop, not using the ability and privilege which they have of looking beneath and within. Yes, they say, we know that there is a time to die. We are born, we live, and then we must die. We know all this. We see it as we go along. We cannot be made more certain of it than we are. We need not be told that there is a time to die.

Thus do mysteries seem trivial because they are constant, and knowledge is slighted because it is near; and thus are men satisfied with mere perception, while they neglect the duty and lose the advantages of reflection. Not that death is to be the only subject of serious reflection; but it stands to reason that, if anything deserves to be pondered, it is the event which terminates our earthly existence, and that if a man will not reflect upon this, the habit of reflection is very much a stranger to his mind.

What is the time of death? Is it any fixed and certain time? Does it come at any particular age? Are all graves of the same length? No. Every hour, every moment, from the instant of birth to the dim limit of the longest life, may be and has been the time of death. Human care and skill, the nurse and the physician, sometimes avert it for a little while; but whether they will so succeed, and for how long, is all unknown. Are warnings given of that time, by sickness, by weakness, by appearances of danger? Sometimes they are and sometimes they are not. No man can tell whether death will strike him with the quickness of lightning, or menace often and delay long.

It follows, then, that the time of death, as it is every and any time within mortal limits, as it cannot with any certainty be governed or regulated or avoided by man, is not in the hands of man. It is not within his knowledge or his power. In whose hands is it?

This becomes the second inquiry. If there be a time to die, and yet that time be wholly uncertain to us, and do not belong to us, to whom does it belong? The question carries the contemplative mind to him who alone reigns in the universal realm of existence, and of whom all life is but the breath. The time of death is dependent on the time of life, and belongs to the Author and Lord of life. "Thou sendest forth thy spirit, we are created; thou takest away our breath, we die and return to the dust." The life of every living man; the death of every mortal, dying man; multitudinous waves, rising, running, sparkling, — declining, sinking, lost, — all unequal, and all momentary, — mysteries to each other, mysteries to themselves, — these are all beneath the eye and hand of him who "sitteth above the water-flood," who ruleth the raging of the deep, and who hears and comprehends the ceaseless murmur of the all-encircling and eternal shore. Life, time, and death, — these are the whole; and the whole is before him, and known to him, and subject to him, and to him only. To him there is no distance and no dimness on this ocean. All is present and all is clear. There is a time to die; the time of change, of the soul's passage, of the second revelation, of the new heavens and the new earth; unknown to all, and infinitely important to all. It is lodged, where alone it could be safely lodged, in the hands of him without whom there would be no life and no death, of him who inhabiteth eternity.

And since the time for man to die belongs not to man, to ignorant man who walketh in a shadow, but to God, with whom is no darkness at all, the thoughtful spirit may discern thus far in its progress, and be glad in discerning it, that whenever this time comes by divine appointment, it comes when it should, and as it should, being altogether wisely and mercifully sent. In this conclusion it will take up its permanent rest; a rest not to be disturbed by the occurrence of cases in which the wisdom and the mercy lie too deep for mortal eye to penetrate, or mortal tongue to explain. And strange indeed it would be, if in the numberless and varying crowd we could see all that is seen by the eternal Disposer, and have nothing left there for the exercise of faith, trust, and submission. But still, if we will consider attentively, we shall perceive in many of the varieties of the time of death wise reasons for each dispensation, and signs of the benevolence of Him in whose hands alone is the time to die. Let us only inquire with a single desire to learn what we can, and an humble conviction that we cannot learn all, that we cannot know everything, and we shall learn full enough for the satisfaction of our reason and the consolation of our heart.

"A time to die." That time is often an early time, coming to the human being as it lies in a new and strange world, all unconscious of this difference between life and death, which so agitates our maturity. The voice whispers in the infant's ear, "Come!" and it obeys, simply, without question or thought. Do we ask why so early a time is appointed? Let us see if there be not some fitnesses in an infant's death. It goes away in a sweet season to the heavenly world. It goes in its innocence, and *with* its innocence, into the pure presence of its Maker. Its robe is unspotted whiteness. Beneath this dress no fear can throb. It need not hide its face with its hands. It appears calmly in the great assembly. It flies confidently to the outspread arms of the Saviour. Without purification, it takes its place with those who have been purified as by fire. The sorrows, pains, cares, and sins of this mortal state have never stained nor touched it. It will be educated altogether in heaven. What is there to offend us in such a time of dying? It is true, that while some are thus early taken, others are left to experience the vicissitudes of earth, to enjoy a little, to suffer a little, to struggle, to sin; and we may ask for the principle of the selection. But we may not be answered. God knows the souls of all his children; we hardly know our own. Some must live on, while others die soon. Let it be granted, as in the faith of immortality it must be, that infancy is a happy time to die, and we may well leave the selection with the Father of spirits. The day will arrive when the principle of the selection will be unfolded. In the light of heaven we shall read and understand it better than we could amidst the shadows of earth.

"A time to die." It is ordained for many that they shall pass through the scenes of multiplied years, and see the various changes which belong to the mortal state. They are not taken in infancy, in childhood, or in youth. The strength of manhood is suffered to flourish and bear its fruit; nor are the leaves shaken from the tree, till in the usual course of nature they are withered. And when these individuals have seen all that life has to show; when they have been continued on earth up to the scriptural boundaries of man's age, or beyond them; and had all their opportunities, all their blessings, and all the common discipline of earth; when their bodily or mental powers, or both, are wearing or worn out; when the people by whom they are surrounded in the world are mostly strangers to them; when those whom they have known and loved best are gone on before them, and they are almost left alone, — is it not their time to die?

Does death come suddenly? And does not the blow save much distress, much lingering anguish, sleepless nights, and wearisome days? Is the shock of a moment to be weighed against the agonies of months, of years? When we fondly think of the happiness which might have been, let us not forget the misery which might have been, had life been continued. When we speak of that which might have been, we speak of that concerning which our ignorance is most profound. God knows what might have been — and God alone.

Again; the time to die is not infrequently deferred till the completion of a long term of sickness and pain; and the subject of divine discipline is ordained to linger on through severe trials of body and mind, now hoping, now fearing, and now hoping again, before the period of release arrives. And is it not a blessed release from such protracted suffering, from such a long captivity? May not death, now if ever, be called an angel, when it bears away on its wings a tired soul to the mansions of rest? As for the suffering itself, is it not the great purifier, the most exalting agent of God's government on earth? And however pure and good the sufferer previous to or at any period of the suffering, how can we ever say that the discipline is needless when we are taught that the Saviour himself was made perfect through suffering?

If the former question be here again put, Why such or such a trial is appointed to one and not to another? it may be replied that one may be tried as efficiently by the absence, as another is by the infliction of pain. It is evident that different individuals require different discipline. Who of us would undertake to order the whole discipline of a fellow-being? Who of us could safely order his own? Why not calmly leave it in the hands of Him who alone can order it wisely; taking care only that we profit by it, whatever it may be. The Omniscient only can understand who ought to be, as he alone can determine who is to be, exercised in this way rather than in that, and taken away at one time rather than another. It is sufficient, if in various times of death we can see manifestations of good.

Yet further, we may perceive in the great uncertainty and variety of the time to die, advantages of a more general character. Consider how strongly, beneficially, and kindly the sympathies of men are engaged and brought into action by the numberless differences in the period and manner of death. If all men were to die at the same time, and in the same way, what a lack of interest there would be, compared with that which is now felt in this momentous subject? How many affections would be left slumbering, which are now roused continually to a full development of their qualities? How monotonous would be the feeling connected with the soul's departure, which is now exhibited in a vast diversity of intense action and passion and influence, informing and quickening the picture of human life, and instituting no small part of human education and probation? If none died in infancy, would not the infant be a less holy being than it now is, and the cause of less holy thoughts in others? If it were regarded as a plant which was necessarily to grow up, and become sturdy, and bear all the storms, and receive all the light and dews and showers of life, would not that inexpressible something, that soft shade in the heart, be wanting, which now flits across it as we bend over the tender bud of being, and think unconsciously of the early frost and the sudden blight? Or should we not miss sadly from the records of human sensation those feelings which arise in the breast at the sight of a child on its bier, —

> "That fairest flower, no sooner blown than blasted:
> That silken primrose, fading timelessly"?

There is a power in such a sight which we cannot do without. It melts down the common pride of life in an instant; and there is no coarseness, no hardness, in the character and heart which it will not, for a time at least, refine and soften.

Sudden death: what call is there among all God's providences so distinctly addressed as this is, to our disposition to procrastinate serious thought and more serious duty? If there were no sudden deaths, all might feel privileged to delay till death could be discerned in the distance. While, on the other hand, if all deaths were sudden, the frequency and commonness of the event would diminish, if not destroy, its startling efficacy.

Death by great and lingering suffering is surely a most afflictive providence; but when I say providence, I mean of course not only a purpose but a wise purpose; and the wisdom is partly manifested in this same appeal which it makes to duty and virtuous sympathies. It is especially in the chamber which has long been devoted to sickness that patience hath its perfect work, and gradually moulds human hearts after the divine likeness, and prepares mortals for immortality. The daily care, the nightly watch, the bitter cup made sweet by the love which proffers it, the constant solicitude on one side, the speechless gratitude on the other, the thousand attentions within from the nearest and most loved, and the kind interest expressed from without by friends and acquaintance, and even strangers; — is all this nothing? We may say, indeed, most naturally, that we would be spared, and will pray to be spared, these severe trials; but human life and society cannot afford to lose them, and the sympathies which attend them; and our better prayer would be, that we may be spared nothing which infinite Wisdom shall see to be conducive to the good of our fellow-beings and our own souls.

Thus it is with the other varieties of the time of death. We shall see particular affections, rare virtues, special charities, springing up everywhere from the field of mortality, each with some characteristic of the spot which produced it. Death runs through all the ages and unites them all. It forms and knits together bonds as strong as those it breaks. It calls virtue out from every change of life, and from every chamber and recess of the heart. And the more affecting it is in its circumstances, the more powerful is its sanctifying influence; for what do we mean, when we declare that a death is a peculiarly affecting one, if we do not mean that hearts are more deeply touched, and good feelings flow forth in a richer flood, than is ordinarily the case?

Beholding these things steadfastly, the reflecting man never feels himself more highly elevated above the cold region of doubt, and above the hoarse cavils of infidelity, than when he is contemplating those very events which are perverted by infidelity to its own support and purposes. He is never more firmly convinced that there is a righteous God than when clouds and darkness are round about him; he never loves God more faithfully, nor adores him more trustingly, than when he is standing in the midst of their shadow.

Nor must it be omitted that much of the benefit consequent on the warnings of death depends on the various and indeterminate seasons of those warnings. If the time to die were one and the same time certainly to all, and that necessarily at an advanced age, in order that the business of life might go on, then childhood, youth, and manhood would be without their several and especial calls of preparation. The general call would sound so faintly from the distance that it would be little heeded. And though it would grow louder as it drew nearer, the ear would hardly measure the gradual increase of its sound. Childhood would not listen to it. Youth would say, there is time enough and to spare; and manhood would declare that there were yet many years in store. The call would be put by, much more commonly than it is now, when each separate age is summoned by deaths of every day's occurrence.

If even now, with all the present variety and multiplied intonations of warning, men are so heedless and spiritually improvident, what would they be were there no such calls to oblige them to pause and think? What a wise provision is this which is constantly throwing in checks among the excesses to which our nature is prone! The young and the beautiful, whom youth makes ardent and confident, — and beauty is so apt to make vain, — cannot always be ardent, confident, and vain. They must receive some lesson, some hint at least, of moderation and humility, with the not infrequent intelligence that those who were as young and beautiful as they have dropped into the tomb. How death tempers the wildness of the world! In times of the most general gayety, there are always contemporaneous sorrows, — some hearts breaking while others are bounding. While we look on gayly thronging crowds, intent on the business, the pleasure, or the wonder of the day, we cannot, — we cannot forget that some houses have their windows darkened and their doors closed, because within them are the sorrowful, the sick, the dead. Thus are our passions modulated. Thus does the low note of sadness run through the music of life, heard in its loudest swells, present in all its variations, uttering its warning accompaniment throughout, and moderating the harmony of the whole.

Finally, does not God teach us, by all the variety and uncertainty of the time of death, that *time* should hardly be brought into the estimate of our great duties and concerns? What is the difference of a few years in the view of the Almighty? By calling us away from earth at all ages, he plainly intimates that it is as nothing. It should be as nothing in our view as in his. Mortal life is but a point. Duty is before us. All sin consists in doing or purposing now that which never should have been done or purposed, and in deferring to some time which we may never see the doing of that which should be done now. "*Now* is the accepted time; *now* is the day of salvation."

September 30, 1832.

SERMON IX.

THE HOUSE OF MOURNING.

It is better to go to the house of mourning than to go to the house of feasting. — *Eccles.* **vii. 2.**

This may doubtless seem a hard saying to many. They will confess that at some future time they may be compelled to go to the house of mourning, but that it is ever better to go there than to the house of feasting is hard for them to conceive.

Appearances sanction their incredulity. The house of feasting beams and sparkles with light. Exhilarating music echoes from its roof. Pleasant company meet in its halls, with smiles and greetings and compliments. Misery and care show not their faces, or not their own faces, within its gates. Its air is perfume; its hues are those of flowers; it is altogether inviting and delightful. On the other hand, the house of mourning is darkened by the outspread wings of the angel of death. Within its shadowed chambers are seated its motionless inhabitants, clad in the sable garments of woe. Its silence is scarcely broken but by unbidden sobs. It seems a cheerless dwelling. Its atmosphere chills the bosom. The countenances of its guests are sad. Pleasure dares not enter its doors. And yet, notwithstanding these appearances, the wise man is right. "It is better to go to the house of mourning than to go to the house of feasting."

He does not say, however, nor does he mean, that mirth and enjoyment are criminal. The Creator did not load the trees and the vines with fruit; he did not people the land, the sea, and the air with their innumerable throngs, in order that man, who is placed in dominion over them, should mortify himself with continual fasting. The Creator did not call into being the endless variety of engaging forms which dwell on earth or float in heaven; nor did he cause the voice of birds and the flow of waters and the rush of winds to make music together, in order that man should have a distasteful ear and a tuneless tongue, and be the only mourner among his joyful creatures. Neither were the light beatings of youthful pulses intended to be all repressed, nor the picturings of the warm imagination to be all condemned, by the frowns of a stern religion. When the proprieties of time and condition invite to enjoyment, and the boundaries of God's law will not be transgressed by enjoyment, religion freely says to us, Enjoy. The text does not proscribe the house of feasting as always unlawful; it does not forbid our going to it; but it tells us that it is better to go to the house of mourning. And it tells us the truth, — truth which admits of satisfactory proof.

It is better to go to the house of mourning, because we obtain more improvement there. More valuable lessons are imparted there than in the house of feasting. Impressions of the most solemn, and not only so, but of the most useful kind, are received there. Our roving thoughts are chastened by the influences of affliction. Our hearts are instructed in the sober wisdom of life. A discipline is administered which befits our condition, and is required by some of the highest wants of our souls.

1. The ways in which this instruction is conveyed to us may be made apparent by reflection. The death of a fellow-being, the departure of one of our friends from the midst of us, is calculated to remind us, more powerfully than almost any other event, of our complete dependence upon God. Can any more important truth than this be borne in upon the mind? And plain as it is, do we not need to have it brought before us in such a manner that we cannot put it by? It is no light thing

that a voice which for years has answered ours in the tones of social intercourse should be struck silent; that a form which has long been familiar to our sight, perhaps one of the daily blessings of our eyes, should pass away and be seen no more. Then it is that we cannot help feeling how frail we are; and how far beyond our own power it is to keep together the circle which is about us, to hinder one after another from dropping out of it, or to maintain our own position within its lessening and uncertain circumference. Who can stay the progress of disease, either of body or of mind? Who can guard against the fatal blows of sudden casualty, which leave us no time for care or for remedies? Who hath power over the spirit to detain the spirit? We are altogether in the hands of God. He takes away the breath which first he gave, and then we die and return to our dust. We depend on him.

2. With this sense of dependence on God, comes humility into our hearts. We cannot but divest ourselves of pride when we gaze on the poor, unconscious, and decaying relics of humanity, and think how quickly and submissively all that lived and moved, was praised and loved and waited upon, and perhaps envied, must gather itself up to become the spoil of a narrow tomb. That this is the end of the body and of its glories, we know. We know

also that the spirit itself is as little able as the body is to choose and command its own life and destiny. That it escapes the fate of the body and survives, we know not till we are told by the eternal word. In all humility, therefore, shall we consider the condition of the spirit, as well as the mortal frame of man, and bless God who has told us what we waited to know, and given us a hope full of immortality.

3. With humility comes a godly fear. We cannot presume that our own life is more secure than was the life of the departed neighbor or friend; and we therefore feel as if we ought no longer to brave, if we have hitherto braved, the divine forbearance, nor delay the preparation which we need. We are moved to look on our neglected lamps, and resolve to fill and trim them, before the door is shut against us and we are left in outer darkness.

4. With godly fear come holy trust and earnest love. God is revealed to us not only as the omnipotent Disposer, who does what he wills with his own, but as the Judge of all the earth, who will do right, and the merciful Father of his children, who chastens us for our benefit, and loves those whom he chastens. Such a Being is not to be feared only, but chiefly and supremely to be loved. And this is our conviction in the house of mourning. It is a fact, and one which deserves to be pon-

dered, that the love of God is often deepest in the midst of affliction, and is of that confiding character which rises superior to all fear except that which is godly, and which may be more distinctly expressed by the term *reverence*.

And now let me pause to ask whether these impressions and thoughts are not in the highest degree beneficial? Do they not correspond with our true condition, as mortal and immortal men? But do they come to us in the house of feasting? If they ever do, it is but rarely and uncertainly. There is no place for them, no time for them, in that house. The sounds of merriment chase them away, except from prepared minds which cannot be long deluded, and from which the convictions of man's real state can never long be absent. But if we are not well established, we are apt to be entirely deceived in the house of feasting. Devoted to immediate enjoyment, we think not whence it was bestowed, nor how soon it may be disturbed and turned into mourning. We become giddy and thoughtless, if not exceedingly vain and presumptuous. Levity may be obstinate as well as wild, and in her own congenial hall she refuses instruction and shuts out wisdom. There is imminent danger that the heart may grow hard in the house of feasting. We are not sensible there of our dependence on God, because we become accustomed to prop ourselves up on all sides by our vanity and self-dependence, and blind ourselves to the weakness and insecurity of such foundations. In the house of mourning our eyes are opened, and we see on what loose and shifting sands, and of what fragile materials, our poor tabernacle is built. We become humble, and in our humility confident and secure.

5. But in pursuing this subject further, we shall perceive that, in addition to the lessons already named, which are taught us in the house of mourning, we are initiated into a discernment of the true worth of our pleasures. We are taught to know that the allurements with which many joys of earth array themselves are very deceptive and transitory. Thus we are made willing to be weaned from them, seeing that they are not so desirable as we once supposed them to be; that they have promised more than they can possibly perform; that they lead to disappointment certainly, and perhaps to shame. We see how devoid of permanent value they are, in their most innocent state, and how worse than worthless when they unfit us, which is their frequent tendency, for the appreciation and inheritance of those real joys which so immeasurably surpass them. We are moved to ask ourselves how we can any longer be devoted to those frivolous pur-

suits which now show themselves in all their frivolousness, and which obtain no approbation either from the judge in our own breast or the Judge who sitteth in heaven. Such an appeal, self-urged, is well fitted to make us pause in a foolish career, and collect ourselves, and weigh folly with wisdom, and vanity with truth, and earth with Heaven.

6. Again; we see in the house of mourning, in a stronger light than perhaps anywhere else, the indispensable importance of a good life. Virtue is revealed there in its true excellence, its fair proportions and character. All doubt of its worth vanishes. All suspicions of its reality are dismissed and forgotten. We are skeptics no more. In seriousness and good faith we pay to it our hearts' homage. We see that the distinction between righteousness and unrighteousness is a real distinction, the most real of any; and that death and friends and the universal will require it to be made and marked. A solemn and settled peace hallows the remains of a righteous man, and follows them to the grave. Respect, affection, and honest gratitude show themselves true mourners. There is nothing forced or affected in the tribute which is rendered. It is the freewill offering of the heart, natural and unbidden. Nothing is more plain and 'sure than the testimony which is given to virtue

in the house of mourning. Nor is there anything more profitable. It confirms those impressions which the world, by much of its intercourse, would weaken. It establishes a faith which the world, by many of its cares and contentions, would wear away. It convinces us that a good name is the most honorable title, and that all the wealth which ever occupied the grasp or the dreams of avarice is dross, is dust, to the riches of an upright, useful, and benevolent life.

7. I could hardly call together and classify all the beneficial reflections which are suggested in the house of mourning. I will only observe, in the seventh and last place, that we are there more than usually disposed to mutual forgiveness and charity. Can we nurture hostile emotions in this house of peace and equality? A soul has gone from it to meet its Judge. It cannot be long before all who are left to mourn or sympathize must follow that soul to the only infallible tribunal. Where will be our petty animosities then? Where the disputes with which we have troubled each other's existence? Where the envyings and strifes, suspicions and evil speakings, of which we have been guilty? Where will they be, and how will they look? Is it right for us, is it safe, to make it our occupation to multiply sorrow in the world? Are

not the unavoidable miseries of life enough in number and in weight, but we must be still increasing the load to others and ourselves? Spirits all in armor sat in the heathen paradise, but they cannot come into the Christian heaven. Can we not forgive offences — we who have so deeply and continually offended? Can the righteous God be merciful, to us unmerciful? Will Christ salute us as blessed children of his Father, who have nourished in our bosoms animosity and revenge against our brethren? These and similar considerations force themselves upon us in the house of mourning. It would be strange if they left us entirely as soon as we departed from it. It is more likely that they will remain with us, at least a little while, and influence our conduct, at least in some degree, when we return into the world.

Valuable are the influences of the house of mourning! It is better that we should go to it than to the house of feasting. The lessons of the one cannot so well be spared as the pleasures of the other. Feasted and filled, unchecked, unalarmed, unsoftened, we are too apt to forget our dangers, our mercies, and our obligations. Earthly desires and passions, temporal objects and interests, claim us as wholly their own. But they seldom dare to go with us to the mansion of bereavement and sorrow.

On its threshold they loosen their grasp and fall back, and we enter in alone, to be spoken to by other monitors, to be sobered and subdued. By the sadness of our countenances our hearts are made better. We see light in darkness, and hear a voice of comfort and joy from the chambers of mourning and death.

July 29, 1827.

SERMON X.

CONSOLATIONS OF RELIGION.

Blessed be God, even the Father of our Lord Jesus Christ, the Father of mercies, and the God of all comfort, who comforteth us in all our tribulation.—2 *Cor.* i. 3.

WELL may we join in this ascription of the apostle, and say, while we contemplate the character and attributes of him whom the Gospel reveals as God, Blessed be God! When we consider what deities they were whom the heathen adored as gods, well may we raise our grateful regards to the God and Father of our Lord Jesus Christ, and say, Blessed be God! And when we reflect how various and severe are the ills of this our mortal life, or when we ourselves are suffering under their infliction, well may we pour out our souls in thanksgiving to the Father of mercies and the God of all comfort, and exclaim, Blessed be God! Thrice blessed be that gracious and most merciful Being, who pitifully beholds our sorrows, and comforts us in all our tribulation. We have need of comfort, we, the feeble sons of men, created of dust, born to mourn and to die, uncertain in our prospects, insecure in our possessions, frail, ignorant, and sinful; and there is not one of us who, in the view of what his situation demands and what Christianity bestows, ought not to repeat, Blessed be God! From him are strength and grace, from him are wisdom and power and victory. He enlightens and inspires, he soothes and saves. He sent his first-born Son to redeem the world; he gives his Holy Spirit freely to those who ask it; he 'has prepared unknown and inconceivable joys for those who love him. Who will not thank and praise his holy name, and, joining with all creatures whose hearts and tongues are inspired by his love, with all the pure and just, with all the sanctified and redeemed, with apostles and martyrs and saints, and with angel and archangel who surround his throne, cry, Blessed be God!

The consolations of religion form a delightful and almost inexhaustible theme of contemplation and discourse. The more they are considered, the more full and abundant do they appear. Let us inquire concerning these consolations, and examine what they really are; and as we increase or refresh our acquaintance with them, we shall very probably come to the conclusion, that, were we to describe Christianity by its most distinguishing characteristic, we should call it a religion of consolations.

If we begin with the first steps and principles of our religion, we shall perceive comfort and consolation broadly and intelligibly marked upon them all. Contemplate the divine attributes; contemplate them one by one. How strongly does each impress the mind with the sentiment of relief and support!

With what magnificent assurance of protection does the idea of God's Almightiness visit the soul, making it certain, beyond suspicion or doubt, that in all its weaknesses and faintings it will be upheld and sustained by that unfailing arm which upholds and sustains the illimitable creation.

How does the attribute of omnipresence encircle us about with safe-conduct and guardianship as with an unassailable host of heavenly angels. How does it encompass us on every side as with a sevenfold shield, at home or in foreign climes, on sea or land, by night and day. It cannot forsake, though all else forsake us; it cannot remove, though the earth be removed. It is with us everywhere, more enveloping than the overarching sky, nearer than the vital air. Who is alone when God is with him? And where can any one be where God is not? " Thou compassest my path and my lying down;" " Thou hast beset me behind and before." Is there not consolation in this surrounding presence, this impregnable defence, this unalienable protection, this watchfulness without fatigue, this adherence without desertion or change, this shadow without darkness, the sheltering and nursing shadow of the Almighty's wings? Does not peace and a confiding sense of security settle down on our comforted hearts, however desponding or afflicted they may have been, when we repeat those trusting words of the Psalmist, "As the mountains are round about Jerusalem, so the Lord is round about his people, from henceforth, even forever?"

"From henceforth, even forever." Yet further treasures of comfort are contained in those last words, which speak of God's eternity. That power which now supports will still support us; that presence which now surrounds and guards will still surround and guard us. Consoling indeed it is to think, that, amidst all which changes, decays, and dies around us, that which is our chief dependence is immutable and immortal, not to be affected by time, not to be disturbed by adversity.

Then there is the attribute of God's omniscience. Great is the consolation to be derived from the thought of that wisdom to which nothing within the bounds of possibility is unknown; which though it often appoints that which afflicts us, always ordains that which is best for us, and can never be mistaken with regard to what we really require, however our own wishes and plans may be contradicted and disappointed.

What is the justice of God but our resort and redress, and the clear, interior light of his throne, even when it is shrouded to our eyes with thickest clouds and darkness? What is it but an assurance that no lasting wrong shall be done, or suffered to be done to us; that our griefs shall have their balance and their recompense; that all seeming inequalities shall finally be smoothed away from the path of Divine Providence, and that no real injuries shall befall us, except those which we inflict upon ourselves?

The attribute of God's loving mercy and kindness is all consolation. It tells us of a Being who has nothing harsh or vindictive in his character; who is always tender and compassionate toward us, though never weakly and injudiciously so; who pities us as a father pities his children, and loves even when he chastens us, and chastens because he loves us.

How can the heart fail to be strengthened and refuse to be comforted, when thus it may repose itself, with all its sorrows, burdens, and incapacities, on infinity, on perfection, on the immutable Rock of eternal ages? Are we sufficiently accustomed to contemplate the divine attributes in this their light of consolation? Should we not attend more to this conspicuous and most adorable characteristic of the whole nature of God? And if we did, should we not bear with a more resigned and contented spirit, not only the great afflictions of life, but the minor troubles and crosses of our condition? Should we not perform our allotted parts more patiently and cheerfully, if we impressed upon our minds such an habitual perception of the Supreme Being, that every feature and mystery of his nature should look down upon us at all times with the expression of benignity, protection, and consolation?

But, consoling as are these views of the attributes of God, Jesus Christ has afforded us yet more comfort by the manner in which he has revealed to us the Father. No one can read the Gospels with attention without being struck by the close and endearing affinity which is manifested there between the Creator and his creatures. The interest which the Great Supreme is represented as taking in us may be called, if it be not too familiar to call it so, strict and personal. Our Saviour does not so much give us general views of the nature of God, as he brings the attributes into immediate contact with ourselves and our fortunes. We behold a God and a Father, who not only supports us, together with the rest of his creation, and provides for us by that wisdom and goodness which are the life and joy of the universe, but who, though the whole globe which we inhabit is but a speck among his works, and we ourselves are so inconstant and frail, actually sets a value upon us, and draws himself as near to each individual soul as if that one soul were the one object of his devoted care, and there was nothing else to share his attention. "Are ye not of more value than many sparrows? Yet not one of *them* falleth to the ground without the knowledge of your Father. The very hairs of your head are all numbered." Expressions of this kind occur so frequently in the Gospels, that they throw a peculiar air of tenderness over them, and cause them to express a particularity of regard in the dealings of God with men, which is one of the most remarkable characteristics of those sacred histories, as it is of the whole Christian scheme. God is represented throughout as our friend; mighty and glorious as in the pictures drawn by the Jewish lawgiver, and the prophets of the old dispensation, but still as our friend, our nearest and best friend.

And this is, in fact, the essence of the doctrine of grace, — the doctrine that God is with us and within us, and always ready, not however interfering with our liberty, to assist and guide us; to suggest to us those thoughts of purity and virtue which are powerful, like spells, to drive away the dark spirits of sin and despair; to inspire us with strength in the hour of weakness, and fortitude in the time of distress, and to shed light through the intricate and gloomy passes of our earthly pilgrimage. What can be more consolatory than to believe, as Christianity would have us believe, that the infinite and eternal God takes this direct interest in our happiness, and that he is, in reality, watching over us and in us, every moment, to mark how we improve the merciful intentions of his discipline, and to aid every good disposition which we may manifest, and every good resolution which we may form? Can that spirit yield, or yield long, before any shock of misfortune, which realizes its intimate union with the Father of spirits? Can that soul remain without comfort in any affliction, which hears within itself the still small voice of God, whispering compassion and peace? Can it sink in the stormy waters when it may call upon its Lord? Can he murmur who can pray? Can the children of the bride-chamber mourn when the bridegroom is with them? When God communes with us, and we with God, does not an elevation, a calm dignity, a holy reliance, follow that communion, which no grief can disturb? Is it fit that the friend and companion of the Almighty should be dismayed at outward and temporary ills? Is it possible that he should? Is it not comfort enough to an humble and contrite and sorrowing heart that the Holy Spirit dwells in it as in a temple? Shall the voice of complaint, shall an accent of distrust, be heard in that consecrated place? Shall fear and despondence appear before that gracious presence? None of these things can be. The Spirit of God is even now, as once at the holiest of baptisms, in the form of a dove. It sheds divine peace in every receiving bosom. It broods over the confused elements of the agitated mind, till darkness becomes light, and chaos is transformed into order and beauty.

With these sources of Christian consolation is connected, and I may say necessarily connected, the Christian doctrine of our immortality. This doctrine is established by deduction from the revealed nature of the Deity, and by the express declarations, confirmed by the actual resurrection, of our Lord Jesus Christ. If anything be true in Christianity, this is true; and it completes those consolations of religion, which without it would be incomplete, faint, and ineffectual. Not much comfort in sorrow would be derived even from a conviction of the constant watchfulness and immediate presence and protection of God, if we could be left to suppose that death wrested us from his guardianship, and put a dark and final close to our connection with his spirit. But after what Christianity taught us of the Creator, we may venture to say it was impossible that it should not have also taught the immortality of his intelligent creatures. It does teach with perfect distinctness that glorious, and, as we may call it, finishing truth, that the existence of man will be commensurate with the existence of God; that the love and the truth and protection which the great Father now exercises toward his children, will lead them through the gate of death; and that the communion which he now holds with them, intimate as it is, will be yet more close and sensible when the Lamb shall walk with their refined and beatified spirits through the bowers of an eternal Eden and the golden streets of the heavenly Jerusalem. This is giving the seal of eternity to all that is compassionate and soothing and exalting in our knowledge of God. This is the key-stone which locks and binds together the grand arch of Christian consolation. When our tears are flowing in calamity, they cease to flow, or flow on without bitterness, when we lift our eyes to that eternal state where they shall all be wiped away. We resign our friends, with hope and comfort in our mourning, because we know that they are not dead but sleeping, and as safe in the arms of God as when they retired to rest on earth after the labors of the day, — perhaps more safe, for passion is hushed and temptation is over. In all our troubles, we shall regard not only the wisdom and kindness of their purpose, but the brevity of their duration; and, with the apostle Paul, " reckon that the sufferings of this present time are not worthy to be compared with the glory which shall be revealed in us."

Such are the consolations of our religion. They are not all, but may be accounted the highest. If we are Christians, they are our consolations, for they cannot be separated from the faith which is in Christ. And how can we have greater and better? What other consolations can we expect or desire when we possess those? There are those, indeed, who, rejecting or slighting these, fly to other sources of comfort. And what are these other? Some wait for the consolations of time, not thinking that, before these can arrive, time to them may be no more. Some trust to a stern, hard, barren endurance. Some fly to a criminal, degrading, stupefying, artificial oblivion. And some even fly to a self-inflicted death. Are these things to be called consolations? If they are, the Christian will never be ashamed or slow to put his own by the side of them and demand a comparison. He will never be backward to put all that ennobles human nature by the side of all that debases, or excites but to depress it; all that unites it with God and heaven and eternity by the side of all that drags it down, and binds it down to sensuality and earth and time and dust. He will stand upon his faith and the consolations of his faith, feeling that he stands upon a height supernal, immovable, everlasting.

May 10, 1829.

SERMON XI.

BLESSING GOD IN BEREAVEMENT.

The Lord gave, and the Lord hath taken away; blessed be the name of the Lord. — Job i. 21.

Can we adopt this sentiment of the afflicted patriarch in our losses and afflictions? Can we say, as well when the Lord takes away as when he gives, Blessed be his name?

It is easy to bless, easy to understand why we should bless, easy to acknowledge that we ought fervently to bless, when the Lord gives; but do we not hesitate, question, doubt, practically refuse to render that offering, when the same Lord who has given, and given all, takes away even but a part? When the field of our possessions lies ample and green before us, and everything prospers which we touch; when we go abroad to successful business, happy meetings, or healthful exercise, and return to a home where every place is filled, every face wears a smile and a welcome, and the whole air is pervaded by comfort and cheerfulness; then we readily allow that we should bless the name of Him by whom all this is caused and given. We may be deficient in gratitude, and in the expression of it, but at the same time acknowledge that we ought to be deeply grateful. When, however, the scene is changed, and our prospect becomes bare and wintry; when distress meets us in the countenances of those we love, casting its shadow on our own countenance and heart; when a place is made void in our dwelling, which we had been long accustomed to see occupied by a form familiar, endeared, bright with kindness and sympathy, — can we be grateful then? Can we bless the name of the Lord then? Why, indeed, should we be grateful, or attempt to be so? What reason is there, we may ask, that we should bless the name of the Lord for affliction and death? Bear, we may; submit, we may; be resigned, we may; — but why should we bless for darkness and for suffering?

Let us answer that question to our reason and our hearts. Taking especially the case of the death of friends, let us consider whether, when we lose even the best, the dearest, there is not occasion for gratitude and thanksgiving. We shall find upon reflection that death is not merely to be held as a loss, either to those who die or those who survive; that death may be significant of gain, much rather than of loss, to the departed and the bereaved; that while it strikes with one hand, it quickens, renews, and transforms with the other; that while it deprives us of some things, it endows us with many more, and more valuable things; and that in this view there is ample cause to bless the name of the Lord when he taketh away, both on account of those who are taken and of those who are left mourning behind.

Death is a benefactor to those who die. For the wisest ends our Maker has implanted within us a strong love of life, of life even in this world; a love of life so strong, that in most cases we could hardly be induced to determine for ourselves the precise moment of rendering it back. And therefore the Maker himself determines that moment for us. And when they die who die in God's own time, it is best for them that they should go away; because it is always best that they should depart this life for whom a higher life is prepared. An exchange of worlds is best even for those who have grossly abused the present life; because it is well known to Infinite Wisdom when the time of probation has been sufficiently extended, when the souls of friends have been sufficiently tried, and when the discipline and awards of another scene should in their deep mystery be commenced. But most surely is the exchange best for the good; for those who have sought the Lord's favor on earth; for those who in meekness and kindness and patience, in sincerity and godliness, have been made " meet to be partakers of the inheritance of the saints in light." Is this world all? Certainly not. They never considered it as all. They never considered it as anything in comparison with the world to come. They knew its glories to be shadows. They felt its joys to be fleeting. They had enjoyed seasons of revelation in which glimpses of heaven had been opened to them, and assurance had been given to their inmost heart that they were born to higher knowledge, and purer bliss, and wider freedom, and closer intimacy with God and their Saviour, than could be afforded them on earth; and therefore it was their faith, their choice, their hope, that they should not be always bound to earth, but should one day be called to rise up and claim their inheritance. In this conviction they had lived. By this conviction they had been helped to bear their trials, and distribute their charities, and extract a sweetness out of every lot. In this conviction they had died; supported in suffering, calm in the last conflict, looking for light, yielding up their souls and their soul's possessions into the hands of God. And now that the conviction has been realized to the holy dead, and that which was hope has become fruition, are they not themselves blessing God for his unspeakable gift; and shall we not join with them in blessing his holy name? As we love them and cherish their memory and revere their piety, we would not contradict them, we would not interrupt the praises they are singing. It is to their heavenly Father and not to a stranger, to their Father's house and not to a strange and doubtful place, that they have gone. It is the Lord and none other, the infinitely wise and gracious Lord, who has taken them away and taken them to himself; and it is but a meet recognition of his wisdom and his goodness, and of the happiness which he has bestowed on those whom we love, that we should say, "Blessed be the name of the Lord!"

And for what did we pray, when we first were made aware that our friends were about to leave us? When we knew them to be, as it is commonly expressed, in danger; when we hung over them in their mortal weakness and extremity, and felt, as we never felt before, how hard it would be to part with them, for what did we pray? In the impulse of our feeling, and surely without blame, we prayed that they might live. God permits us so to pray, both for ourselves and for our friends, because we have much to do in this life and much to learn and much to receive; and the domestic relations are very dear, and the household affections are very strong. We prayed, as we hung over them, that they might live. And the prayer was granted, — not to our desire, but to our need, — not to the temporal meaning of our words, but to their better and eternal meaning. A life was granted them, pure, free, safe, real, unlike that " death, called life, which us from life doth sever," — life in a better world, a fairer country, a healthier clime. No cold is there, nor blight; no tears, no pride, no penury. Life has there a clearer and fuller meaning than it can have here. The epithets, dim, uncertain, troubled, transitory, can no more be applied to it. No longer can it be compared to a vapor, a dream, the path of an arrow, a pilgrimage in the desert. It is life eternal and blessed. This was the life which was given, instead of that which was asked. "He asked life of thee, and thou gavest it him, even length of days, forever and ever." One upward thought, one Christian reflection, will show us, that, when our righteous friends have been taken away by commission from above, we should say, for their sakes, " Blessed be the name of the Lord!"

Should we not also say it for our own sakes? For what should we bless the Lord more sincerely, more fervently, than for the confirmation of our religious convictions; for the increased purity and depth of our best affections; for the enlargement of our experience, the discipline of our passions, the growth of our spiritual nature? And when is all this vouchsafed as it is in the time of bereavement? Then it is, if ever, that we gain a large supply of life's true wisdom, and are convinced that it is the principal thing. Then it is, if ever, that our hearts are strongly stirred, and the fountains of feeling pour forth all their waters. Even if we have long been established and settled in the principles of a holy faith, yet the worth of those principles is brought home to us as it was never before, acquiring a new addition of personal and practical weight, and manifested to our very sight and touch. And if, unhappily, the world has hitherto been "too much with us"; if fashion has been doing its utmost to make us frivolous; if collision with men and their selfishness has been hardening our sensibilities, and tending to render us skeptical concerning spiritual interests and heavenly treasures; there is something in the season of domestic bereavement which suddenly melts away the ice which has been curdling round our hearts, and sets our better nature free. Shall not the name of the Lord be blessed for this? Oh that the touch of his hand and the lesson of the hour might abide! But too often the good impression of the time is suffered to fade away, and the world to resume its power, and the ice again to curdle round the heart.

If it should be so, the fault is only ours. Blessed be the name of the Lord for the word which he has spoken, whether we have heard or whether we have forborne to hear, whether we have remembered or whether we have forgotten it.

He teaches us plainly, by taking away our righteous friends, that there is a preparation to be made, and that our friends have made it. He causes us to feel that virtue and godliness are the greatest gain that can possibly be gathered; that wealth is not valuable, that earthly renown is not to be mentioned, that learning is folly, that genius itself is emptiness, compared with Christian holiness. Those may be and have been abused, and turned to the worst and lowest uses; but this is always pure and incorruptible. By those we may have been hurt and wronged, but never by this, which has never been near us but to help us and soothe us. Those cannot pass beyond the grave, and must be left on earth where they belong; but this passes with the spirit, holiness passes with the emancipated spirit, through the gates of death to the bosom of the Father. The Lord has taught us what is truly enduring. He has taught us impressively and at home. Blessed be his name!

A check has been interposed in our path. A shadow has been thrown across it. The sun of life has set for this day, and the darkness which comes down invites us to reflect on our way, and reveals to us the stars of heaven. It is a check which we would not have invited, a darkness which we would not have chosen; but our spirit within us acknowledges, in its own more sobered state, in the multitude and fulness of its retired thoughts, in its gentler tone and more humble and charitable dispositions, the uses of the ordination which has been laid upon us. Taught by sorrow, we know better how to sympathize with the sorrow of others, and can better estimate the value of others' sympathy. This truth is learned in stillness. And hopes break out upon us from above, of which we hardly knew the glory before; and we learn that the day has one sun, but that the night has many. This truth is learned in darkness. The Lord is teaching us by bereavement to be kinder to our brethren and more faithful to himself. Blessed be his name!

But even if we should not be able distinctly to specify and enumerate to ourselves the benefits which are derived to our souls in the season of bereavement, there is always one religious inference which we can draw, of the simplest nature, and calculated to be of the greatest service. The Lord gave us our friends. He gave us those dear ones whose communion with us has constituted so great a part of our happiness. For what purpose did he give them, and with what intention? Certainly for our benefit, and to do us good, and because he loved us. This we know from our experience. Why then did he take them away? Not with a different purpose surely. It is the same Lord. He did not give with one intention, and take away with another which is contrary to it. He did not give to do us good, and take away to do us harm. Now, as before, there is love and love only in his heart toward us. Let us feel that God is always love, and can be nothing else, and we can say, even though blind and in tears, Blessed be his name!

With the Gospel in our hands, with Christ to guide, with his saints to cheer us, let us try to be at least as elevated in our views, at least as spiritually-minded, as that afflicted and chastened patriarch whose words we have borrowed; at least as wise and calm as that old man of a long departed age, lord of tents and flocks, sitting in twilight, before the day-spring from on high had risen on those eastern plains. If he, in the time of dimness, could see cause to utter that beautiful form of faith and submission, we surely may repeat it in light. As to life and its essential relations, they are the same now as they were then; and death and its circumstances are the same. The messengers of sorrow and calamity came to him one after another, announcing bereavement upon bereavement till he found himself stripped and destitute; and so, in our own day, does one affliction often press hard on the footsteps of another, with a suddenness and rapidity which confuse and bewilder us. But it is the Lord of life and death, eternally enduring from age to age, who sent those calamities to him, and who sends repeated afflictions to many in these latter days. The only difference is, that faith has a clearer vision now, and stands on a stronger foundation. The grave is as near, but heaven is nearer, because the grave has been opened by the Son of God. And more fervently, and with a more cheerful heart, should we, in our sorrows, bless the name of the Lord, because he is called by us the God and Father of our Lord Jesus Christ.

SEPTEMBER, 28, 1838.

SERMON XII.

REMEMBRANCE OF THE RIGHTEOUS.

The righteous shall be in everlasting remembrance. — *Psalm* cxii. 6.

The earth holds many more inhabitants than those who walk upon its surface in material shape. The human forms which at any given period dwell on it visibly together, are but a part of its mighty population. Graves and tombs hide its dead from sight, but not from memory; from the outward, but not from the inward eye. Neither the green turf nor the salt wave can effectually separate the dead from the living; the dead, who live, from the living who must die. Generations of men succeed each other, but do not wholly pass away. Multitudes of those who were, remain to the thoughts and affections of the multitudes who are, and, by the mind's survey and computation, to be numbered with them. "The righteous shall be in everlasting remembrance."

And as death is not oblivion, we may be led to hope, even from this fact, that it is not destruction. The dead live on earth. The soul, by a natural and necessary power, preserves them from annihilation. Is not this a suggestion at least, that they actually, consciously live? Memory is an intimation, a shadow, a kind of vision of immortality. The spirit of man refuses to consider the old times as wholly blank and void, as utterly silent. It sees forms which have ceased to be corporeal; it hears voices which for long years have not spoken with tongues. It fills the past with the life and intelligence which once existed, and which it will not suffer to become extinct. Does not the soul thus point out and claim for itself its immortal affinities? Are not here a strong and holy union and consent between memory, which looks back and tells of that which is gone, and faith and hope, which look forward and proclaim that which is coming? It seems to me that the acts of memory are of the nature of miracles, continually worked for the conviction of unbelief. Why may not faith and hope raise the dead when memory does raise them?

"The righteous shall be in everlasting remembrance." It is they who come to the resurrection of life. It is they only who are remembered with a holy, living, embalming remembrance. Others are remembered with a fatal remembrance, — remembered to be doomed; according to that scripture which saith, "The memory of the just is blessed; but the name of the wicked shall rot."

When we come to survey them, how vast are the numbers of those who live in memory. They emerge from the dimness of the primitive generations; they come from the farthest isles; they start up from among heaps of ruins which once were cities; they rise from old battle-fields, from village churchyards, from the depths of seclusion, from the bottom of the sea. They fill the earth with immortal souls. Their memory is blessed. The present generation, as it names their names and recalls their virtues, would not and cannot divest itself of the impression that they are in being, and that itself is not here alone, but surrounded by an innumerable company.

I. The world has a memory, whereby it treasures up the names and deeds of those who have been its lights, its ornaments, its benefactors. It holds in everlasting remembrance those who, while they walked on earth, walked with God, and served their age. It remembers the sages who have framed wise and equal laws, who have originated and carried into effect useful inventions, who have been instrumental in banishing cruel or degrading superstitions, who have taught the truth in love. It remembers those noble spirits who have been found faithful among the faithless, pure among the corrupt, thoughtful among the thoughtless; those martyrs who have laid down their lives for truth and freedom; those great and good men, who in any and every way, by resisting oppression, by relieving distress, by emancipating the prisoner, by instructing the ignorant, by publishing peace and salvation to those who are near and those who are afar off, have contributed to the intelligence, virtue, and happiness of their race. As the world grows wiser and better, it remembers with increasing regard those who were once persecuted by it for righteousness' sake; it remembers and blesses those whom it once reproached and made to suffer wrongfully, because they were more just and righteous than itself; while it permits rottenness to creep insensibly over the names of the wicked, however proud and renowned they may once have been.

II. The number of those who live in remembrance increases before us, when we consider that the several nations and smaller communities of the earth have each a memory for those who are seldom or never mentioned or known beyond their respective boundaries. How many are the learned and the holy, how many the gifted and benevolent and devoted, who are held in high honor and long remembrance in those sections of the globe where their talents and virtues have been exhibited, and their duties have been done. Names are household words in one country or district, which have not reached to another, and which yet are altogether worthy of their local shrines. Every city has its list of scholars and orators and philanthropists and eminent men. Every village can reckon its patriarchs, its teachers, its saints. The images of all these occupy their wonted places. Their spirits are attached to their familiar haunts, and are seen among them. And thus their good influence remains, after their good work is accomplished. Much of the virtue of the present generation is derived from the remembrance of the righteous departed; for the remembrance of the righteous is a remembrance of righteousness, of that which caused them to be remembered. It comes clothed with holy associations, which are all the more holy as the garment of the flesh has been removed. It increases the number of virtuous thoughts. It may be brought to the aid of virtuous resolutions. It is a pure memorial, which operates as an inducement and encouragement to purity, and as a check upon impure suggestions and unworthy conduct. It is indeed one of the richest portions of that inheritance which is left by one generation to another. And thus not only is the memory of the just blessed, but they who cherish it are blessed by it. It blesses as it is blessed. Happy is that people who have many righteous to remember, and who preserve the remembrance of them with care and reverence. And happy are they who, convinced that all fame is poor compared with the remembrance of the righteous, make it their chief ambition to secure that remembrance. Whatever some may think, it is the only remembrance which shall be everlasting, — the only remembrance which contains the elements of life and honor and blessing for evermore.

III. As dwellers in this world for a season, as pilgrims passing through it in our turn, we remember those who have passed on before us, and who live in the world's memory. As members of subordinate communities, we remember the names which are sanctified in those communities. But these are far from being all who are remembered. Each circle of friends, each separate family, has a memory; and the forms which are retained by it are, of all others, the most distinct, the most vivid, and the most dear. What numbers, what numbers are they of whom the world has never heard, and never will hear, but who live forever in the bosoms of kindred. Beneath every domestic roof there are more than are counted by the stranger. Spirits are there whom he does not see, but who are never far from the eyes of the household. He does not see the sprightly child, who once was there in mortal health and beauty; but the child is yet there in spiritual presence before the vision of father and mother, and wherever they may go, will go with them. He does not see the venerable form which once sat there in placid love and dignity; but it has not departed from that house; son and daughter behold it; it looks on them with wonted kindness, and speaks to them still the words of counsel. He does not see the devoted wife, whom once he might have seen there, the presiding spirit of order and comfort and peace, ruling her children with gentleness and discretion, and causing her husband to realize what a refuge and sanctuary and heaven on earth is home; but from that home she has not wholly departed, nor will ever depart, for her remembrance is there perpetually. Though the body has been borne for the last time from its doors, her spirit remains in its influence over the affections and the deportment of the living. To them she utters her voice, and by them she is heard; and the husband is not wholly alone, and the tender minds of the children are moulded insensibly by the very name of her who watched over their infancy. There is something of this in every house which love and virtue entitle to the name of home, in every family where mortality has taught the lessons of immortal faith and hope. Steps are on the stair, but not for common ears; and familiar places and objects restore familiar smiles and tears, and acts of goodness, which are seen by memory alone. Who shall enumerate the blessed multitude of those who, dead to all on earth beside, live always in the hearts of those who knew them and loved them.

The body may be far distant, but the spirit is brought near by remembrance, and dwells ever at home. The mortal remains of a friend may be covered by a foreign soil, and strange and heedless feet may tread on the spot where they lie; but the soul returns to its own country, and communes with its own kindred. That which was corruptible may have been committed to the deep, and the track of the receding vessel be the only path to the place of its sepulture; but the waves cannot roll over the uplifted and imperishable spirit. He who was absent, is present. The members of his family behold him unchanged.

IV. I have said that the world has a memory; that each community of men has its memory; that each family has its memory; and that by all these the righteous are kept in everlasting remembrance. But families are broken up, and dispersed, and obliterated; nations rise and fall, and their memory perishes with them; and the world itself shall grow old and languish and die. What then should we be, and what would even righteousness avail, if there were no other memory but that of our friends, our country, or the world? But there is One who will endure, though the earth and the heavens shall perish, — the First and the Last, — of whose years there shall be no end. He remembers his creatures with an all-comprehending and eternal memory; and especially he remembers those who remember and put their trust in him. Memories on earth go out, one after another, like lamps when there is no one to feed them; but in heaven they are more lasting than the stars, and they burn in fadeless lustre around the throne of the Almighty. "Our days are gone like a shadow, and we are withered like grass; but thou, O Lord, shalt endure forever, and thy remembrance throughout all generations." Blessed hope, glorious truth! the righteous shall be in everlasting remembrance with God. And if he remember, what does it matter if every one else forget? Some there may have been so humble, so solitary, so destitute, that they have left none behind them to mourn or remember them; and many there have been of whose existence the world, and all who are in the world, become gradually unconscious. But they were righteous, and they stand full in the remembrance of God. And to be in the remembrance of God, what is it but to be in his presence? To be in the remembrance of the Eternal One, what can it be but to live before him in his light and glory and joy eternally? Here, in the strictest, as well as highest sense, everlasting remembrance must be everlasting life. How earnestly, then, we should strive ourselves, and persuade all to live, not in the show and pride of a dreaming life, but in the remembrance of God! "Then they that feared the Lord spake often one to another; and the Lord hearkened and heard it, and a book of remembrance was written before him for them that feared the Lord, and that thought upon his name. And they shall be mine, saith the Lord of hosts, in that day when I make up my jewels; and I will spare them, as a man spareth his own son that serveth him."

Let our names, O Lord, be written in that book of remembrance, among those who fear thee and think upon thy name! Let us be thine, O Lord of hosts, in that day when thou makest up thy jewels; and spare us, as a man spareth his own obedient son!

DECEMBER 14, 1834.

SERMON XIII.

NOTHING WITHOUT CHRIST.

For without me ye can do nothing. — *John* xv. 5.

Peculiar solemnity attends this declaration of Jesus to his disciples, from the circumstance of its being pronounced among his last words, on the night before his death. The occasion of the Supper, which he instituted at that time, probably suggested the form of the context, in which he compared himself to a vine, the Father being the husbandman, and his disciples to the branches. " As the branch cannot bear fruit of itself, except it abide in the vine, no more can ye, except ye abide in me. I am the vine, ye are the branches. He that abideth in me, and I in him, the same bringeth forth much fruit; for without me ye can do nothing." His assurance to them is, in all this portion of the discourse, that, as the branches derive their life and nutriment through the vine, or stock, so do they derive their spiritual life and nutriment from him; that, as the branches are connected with each other by their common junction to the vine, so will their brotherly love continue and be perfected only by their constant union with him and his love; that, as the branches could produce no clusters if separated from the vine and deprived of its juices, so neither could they bring forth the fruits of the spirit and the works of their heavenly mission, except through direct supplies of grace from him and his righteousness.

"For without me ye can do nothing." This is the conclusion. The disciples felt its truth and its weight. They felt it afterwards even more strongly than they did then. When their Master, their wise and gentle and all-suffering Master, who had been with them so long and loved them so well, was taken from them, they felt, in their desolateness, that they could indeed do nothing without him. When they were left to themselves, to act for themselves, they felt, in the conviction of their own personal destitution and dependence, that they could indeed do nothing without him; that if they were to proceed at all, they must proceed as his apostles, in the way which he had pointed out; that if they were to receive supernatural aid, they must look for it through his promises; that if they were to act with any unity of purpose and affection, and any concentration of will and effort, they must be united in attachment and subjection to him, their living Head; that if they were to teach and reform the nations and move the world, they must do so only through his truth, his wisdom, and his dying and redeeming love. What *could* they do without him? By him they had been chosen from the world, and made the companions of his wondrous life; from him they had received all the knowledge and power which caused them to differ in any way from common men; through him they had been cheered with that immortal faith, without which they would have been of all men the most miserable; through him had been imparted to them the gifts and comforts of the Holy Ghost, tongues of fire and hearts of constancy, according to his faithful engagement. What *could* they do without him?

Can we suppose the attempt on their part of acting independently of their former Master, and without a primary reference to his assistance, his doctrines, and his commandments? How would they have appeared as instructors and reformers, not to say apostles, each one with his own theory of religion and morals; following the path of his own impulses; borrowing at one time from the philosophy of Greece, and at another from the philosophy of Rome; taking exception to this and that declaration of Jesus; making abatements here and there from the supremacy of his authority; saying but little of his death, and less of his resurrection; passing lightly over, and suffering to fade from their memory, the events of his life and ministry, as things merely external and historical, and not sufficiently spiritual; neglecting to commemorate him, according to his dying request, in the communion of bread and wine; speaking and teaching seldom or never in the name of Christ; putting no trust in his strength or promises? How would they have appeared? What would probably have been the result and effect of their instructions; and what the character of the Christianity which they would have left to us?

But they are wronged by the very supposition. Merely to suppose that they could have chosen to act thus, seems to be doing injustice to those faithful disciples,— injustice alike to their affections and their understanding. They knew that without their Master they could do nothing, and they had no thought or desire to do anything without him. Their acts and their epistles show that Christ was ever on their tongues and ever in their hearts. In his name, and relying on his aid, they went forth into the world, preaching Christ the power of God and the wisdom of God, and declaring that there was no other name through which men might be saved. What he had delivered to them they taught to others. They preached his word, his cross, his resurrection. In him they lived, in him they labored, in him they suffered, and in him they triumphed. They did nothing without him. The consequence was salvation to themselves, and salvation to the world.

The case of the apostles is our own case, my friends, with the exception only of the peculiarities of their situation and mission. Without Christ we can do nothing; nothing in the concerns and ways of our highest moral life; nothing in relation to those objects of faith and hope and duty which he came to render clear and sure to the spirits of men. Without him, the soul is left without its support and guide. Without him, the soul struggles, but accomplishes nothing; meditates, inquires, searches, but is made certain of nothing; pursues various ends, but arrives at nothing. Without "the true light," it gropes and wanders in the ancient darkness; without "the true bread," it hungers and faints; without "the true vine," it brings forth no fruit.

Perhaps we are not aware, or do not sufficiently consider, how much we owe to Christ in the insensible participation of those general benefits which have been bestowed by Christianity on the community in which we live. These general benefits are the aggregate of the sentiments and convictions which, in every age, individuals have derived immediately from Christ, and have preserved and imparted, and which have contributed to form what may be called a general knowledge and a general faith, the sum of which is great, though not to be precisely estimated. We participate in these salutary influences, we inhale like common breath these airs of Paradise, without being conscious of their real source; but their source is Christ. A large amount of Christian knowledge and Christian principle is abroad, not assuming a distinctive name, and so diffused in various forms of communication and instruction, and through all the relations of life, and all its hours, from those of childhood forward, that it necessarily reaches and affects every one, modifying in greater or less degree his thoughts, feelings, conduct, condition. Of this influence we are unconscious, for it is in a manner insensible. But inquiry will soon reveal both its reality and its origin; and we act an ungrateful part, if, having enjoyed its benefits, we ascribe them to ourselves, or to the progress of our human nature, and claim an independence on Christ, in the strength of those advantages which Christ, and none other, has in fact bestowed. In no state of society, anywhere, before Christ came into the world to enlighten it, should we have participated in those advantages; and in no country or nation where Christ is unknown, could we be partakers of them now. To him we owe them, and to him we should refer them. Opinions, sentiments, and hopes, views of the present and the future, motives of action, thoughts of duty and of God, familiar to us as the faces of home, always known to us as if they were born with us, are yet not ours, by right of nature, but his, our Saviour's, and ours only by grace. It is not without his help, not without his original suggestion, that we think these common household thoughts are moved by these apparently natural impulses. Even these are from him. Even here we can do nothing without him. Out in the world, acting with its citizens, walking with its people, reasoning with its reasoners, what is best and strongest in us comes primarily from Christ.

But this is only the first and most general view of our dependence. When we turn to an examination of ourselves and our religious state, in direct and immediate relation with the Saviour, it is then that the conviction is most forcibly impressed upon us, that we can do nothing without him. We arrive at our most intimate, consoling, and elevating knowledge of God the Father, through his Son Jesus Christ. We acquire our simplest, clearest, kindest, and most practical views of duty from him and his life. We learn from him distinctly, what is the acceptable worship and service which man is required to render to his Maker. We know through him and his resurrection, what we could not otherwise have known, whatever we might have hoped, that we are immortal, that we shall live after death and forever. By him we are brought into connection with that bright community of angels and sainted spirits, whose voices we hear on earth by faith, cheering us in our journey, and inviting us to the enjoyment of their society and his own, everlastingly in heaven. While we continue with him, studying his life, meditating on his image, listening to his words, imbibing his spirit, we are possessed with all this knowledge, faith, and power; but away from him and without him, where is it to be found, and what can we do? I confess I know not. If I could dismantle my own heart of all traces and memorials of the Saviour, I know that I should be startled at its emptiness and desolation, and, finding in it but little to repair the melancholy loss, be forced to weep in despair over the ruin I had made. And as empty and solitary as my heart, should I find the domains of ancient philosophy and religion. What should I get there but evil mixed up with good, hope glimmering through darkness, and doubt enfeebling all conclusions? Whom should I discover there, among the best and greatest, who could give to my soul that divine security, that heavenly rest, which is so freely offered by Christ, or who could reflect upon my soul that image of purity and holiness which is revealed in the person of Christ? Every system and treatise into which I might look, every face to which I might turn, would seem to ask me, in wonder, why I came to them for that divine authority, purity, and beauty which they lived too early to see, and for that light beyond the grave which they were searching for so anxiously themselves.

Christ is my companion and guide in the path of my mortal life, through all difficulty and danger, always ready and efficient with his counsel, sympathy, and assistance. Am I in doubt concerning some question of duty, some rule of conscience? I have only to refer to his word or his example, and my course is plain. Am I in peril from some lurking and besetting temptation, almost irresistible from the appeals which it makes to my weaker nature? One glance at his pure countenance, one touch of his invigorating hand, and I am my better self again, and have strength to spurn the assaulter away. Have I neglected to seek my helper in season? have I wandered from the right way? and do I at length see and deplore my fault, confused and ashamed?

I hear his voice, not repelling me by harsh accents, but gently accepting my repentance, and inviting my return. Is my heart deeply pierced by disappointment or any grievous sorrow? or is my flesh troubled by racking pain? I look to the Man of Sorrows, to the suffering Lamb of God, to his bleeding temples, to his agonizing cross; and his wounds are the healing of mine. Do I stand by the bedside of a departing friend, feeling that I am wretched, and that when the final breath is breathed I shall be more wretched still, but striving to restrain my tears, in the fear of disturbing the last moments of one I love? Christ is with me where I stand, assuring me that my friend will not die, but only sleep, and that I shall meet him again, and be parted from him no more. I bless the sacred accents, and my tears gather silently, and my bosom is calmed. And so when I come myself to the brink of the river, Christ will be with me then, who has been with me always, and the warmth of his dear and glorious presence will dispel the chilly vapors, and he will lead me safely through. What then could I do without him? How can I live, how can I die, without him?

Master! to whom shall we go? thou hast the words of eternal life. Thou hast said we can do nothing without thee. Son of God, it is true! Saviour of men, it is true! Thou art the vine, we are the branches. Our spiritual life is nourished and invigorated from thee; and if we bear fruit, it is because we abide in thee, and still receive the vital streams which flow from thee alone.

Is it necessary that any one should be guarded against the error of inferring, that because without Christ we can, in a spiritual sense, do nothing, therefore with him we are relieved from all responsibility of exertion, and have nothing to do for ourselves? I should hope not. Have we not yet to maintain our connection with him, yet to follow where he leads, yet to make use of the knowledge, and yet to apply the power which he furnishes? If an artist place in the hands of a pupil all the most finished instruments which are proper to his art, and afford him all the instruction which is needful to secure his advancement in it, and give him, moreover, the promise that he will always take an interest in his success, and be near to advise and direct him, has the pupil therefore nothing to do? Are the instruments which have been furnished him to lie unemployed on his table, and is he to fold his hands, and sit down, and say that all is now complete, and he is perfect in his profession, or else deplore his inability, and wait for something more to be done for him? Everything has been done for him which could be done for a responsible being; for all the means have been imparted to him for the needed end. And yet he has, in the other view of the subject, everything still to do. He has still to practise his art with industry; still to study its principles with diligence; still, by his own indefatigable labor, to make himself a proficient in its mysteries and applications. If he do not this, his own proper part, he sadly mistakes and neglects his duty; and no boast of perfection, or complaint of incompetency, will avail to excuse him. It is so with the Christian, who is the pupil of Christ. His Master has done everything for him, by instruction, by example, by impression, by the aids of his grace and spirit; and yet the pupil is, for this very reason, in the condition which requires his own most faithful and grateful exertions to improve and exercise these heavenly endowments. It is not enough for him to say that his Master is perfect, and he trusts wholly in his Master's perfection and merits. Certainly he ought to trust in his Master's perfection and merits, without whom he is nothing; but not in such a way as to render him morally idle, or lead him to indulge the erroneous thought that anything can be done for him which it is his own special part to do for himself, or that he can be found in his Master's image, without taking some pains to copy his example and obey his directions.

Without Christ, our Lord and Saviour, we are nothing. Therefore most gratefully should we acknowledge our dependence, and the invaluable gifts of knowledge and power and comfort which we owe to him, and most earnestly, also, should we endeavor to make a worthy disposition of his bounties, in the temper and actions of an answering love and obedience. Thus, and thus only, will his strength become effectually ours; his consolations our rejoicing; his merits our salvation. The branches will remain on the vine, never to fall or wither. Our life will be like his, because nourished from his, divine and eternal.

NOVEMBER 28, 1841.

SERMON XIV.

PERPETUITY OF CHRIST'S KINGDOM.

And of his kingdom there shall be no end. — *Luke* i. 33.

THESE words are a part of the angelic annunciation to the blessed Mary. They contain a promise that the reign of the princely Son, who was to be born of her, should be perpetual. There is every probability that the promise will be gloriously fulfilled. Beside the trust which we repose in the declarations of the Scriptures, of which there are several of the same import with our text, we have the history and experience of the past, the tendencies of the present, the prospects of the future, and the nature itself of Christianity, to assure us that the kingdom of the Messiah will be an everlasting kingdom; that the name of Christ will forever be glorified; that the precepts and doctrines of Jesus will never fail of their influence nor be robbed of their reverence; that of the power of pure and undefiled religion, and the reign of God and heaven, there will be no end.

And chief of these we have the nature of Christianity to give us the assurance of its stability. This assurance is proclaimed by its own immortality. And it is immortal, because its subject-matter, because the elements which go to compose it, because the foundations on which it is reared and supported, are all immortal and eternal. When therefore the question is put, why there will be no end of Christianity, the answer from a consideration of its nature is, because there will be no end to virtue, to faith, to reason, to hope, to fear; no end to the aspirations of men after the highest good; no end to heaven and to the idea of an immense and holy future; no end to the being, the government, and the acknowledgment of God. Christianity does not consist in objects which are outward, and therefore liable to be worn and to be changed; it does not rest on things which are passing away; but it consists in and rests upon those thoughts, sentiments, affections, principles, and objects, which are rooted permanently within, and seated permanently above, and which cannot wear out, nor be weakened, nor pass away.

Christianity teaches the nature and character of God. The idea of God is in fact the animating spirit of the system, without which it would be dead, or nothing. Will the idea of God, the idea of one, supreme, perfect God, ever be obliterated from the human mind? Once imprinted there, is it likely that it will ever be obliterated? Can any idea be presented to the mind, which comprises so much that is elevating and comforting to its weakness, and congenial and satisfying to its noblest moods and most enlarged capacities? Is it to be supposed that the mind will ever grow so sluggish and careless, or become so deranged, as to be content to lose, or anxious to cast away from its keeping and remembrance, that thought which, of all thoughts, raises, strengthens, expands, and consoles it the most, — that thought which may be called its own apotheosis? If man cannot resign the idea of God, then, so far, Christianity is safe and permanent. But will there ever be any change or improvement in the idea' of God, such as Christianity offers it, so that Christianity in this respect will be superseded? Not unless an advance can be made upon perfection. Not unless unity can be made more than absolute; power mightier than Almighty; wisdom greater than infinite; and love more full, more free, more constant than love itself, without limit, without alloy, without restraint, and without end. Not unless God can be named by a name dearer than that of Father, or invested with a character nearer and more benignant and engaging than that of paternal. Not unless a providence can be imagined more majestic than that which orders all things in heaven and earth, or more careful and watchful than that by which the hairs of our heads are numbered. That such is the idea of God, as given in the Christian Scriptures, is capable of demonstration. That any improvement can be made on such an idea, is not capable of being conceived. The effect of any improvement or purification of the divine idea, as it exists among men, will forever be to bring it nearer to that idea as it is expressed in the Christian records, and not to produce any alienation or superiority, which is impossible.

I conclude, then, that, as the human mind cannot part with the idea of God, which is required by its wants and is kindred to its constitution; that, as the mind is aided and elevated by this idea, on the principle of a constant progression, of which it is the urging and expanding power or spring; and that, as all advancement in this direction is an approach toward the Christian standard, which, from its perfection, cannot be surpassed,—Christianity will be perpetual. Its light cannot be put out, for God is its illumination. It cannot die, for the spirit which penetrates and informs it, and the life which invigorates and quickens and preserves it, is God.

The same conclusion is to be drawn, secondly, from the morality of the gospel. Of the kingdom of Jesus there shall be no end, because of the reign of virtue, of holiness, there shall be no end. The principle of virtue is a conservative principle. The absence of virtue from any system which is intended for the mind and heart of man, is an infallible mark of its decay. It is a spot which will spread into corruption, and bring on debility, and terminate in death. The system may prosper for a while, and its prosperity may be sudden, but so will be its decline; like insect-stung fruit, which is forced into premature and fair seeming ripeness by the poison which spoils it. The morality of the gospel may challenge, and for eighteen centuries has challenged, examination. The result has been that it has approved itself more and more to the esteem and reverence of men. Unbelievers themselves have acknowledged — those unbelievers, I mean, who have mind and feeling and principle, and do not descend into the rank of mere scoffers — that the morality of the Christian system is purer and brighter and loftier than that of any other. Nor do I mention this fact because I consider Christianity at all indebted or beholden to infidels for their courtesy, which, though it would not reject, it may safely spare; nor because I regard an unbeliever as in the least degree a better judge of what is good and what is true than a believer. Not at all. But I mention it, because the evidence of unbelief is extorted evidence, and unites strongly with that which is more willingly rendered; and because this testimony to the high virtue of our religion is just so much unwitting testimony to something more,—even to its divine origin, to its complete truth, and to its endless stability. The acknowledgment that, from the northern corner of Palestine, from despised Nazareth, came forth a system, before the moral superiority of which all other systems must bow, is the acknowledgment of a fact very near to a miracle. It is also the acknowledgment of its perpetuity. Perfect holiness is of itself perpetuity. It is the conservative principle, without any mixture or alliance with sin, which is the great element of corruption and dissolution. Every voice, therefore, from every quarter, which confesses the pure morality of the religion of Jesus, joins with that of the angel who saluted his virgin mother, in proclaiming that of his kingdom there shall be no end.

And the morality of the gospel in its completeness is yet but imperfectly understood and partially felt. It is unfolding itself in new power to the understandings and hearts of men; and this its progressiveness is a token of perpetuity. The peculiar and distinguishing portion of the Christian morality is only beginning to be felt and practised as its author intended it should be. The self-denying and peaceful virtues have not yet shown half their power, nor effected half their triumphs. But they are going on with a march as sure as that of time. Men are coming daily nearer to a just perception of their value and beauty, and their gracious influence on human happiness. How far off men were from this just perception when the angelic song of peace and goodwill was sung to the shepherds of Bethlehem! how far off, when the great and blessed Teacher himself preached glad tidings to the poor! So far off, that it was the inculcation of these virtues, so disappointing to passion and pride; it was this preaching to and for the poor and oppressed, so incomprehensible to prejudice and vainglory, which brought him to the cross. Yes, the preaching of the gospel to the poor was the initial cause which, through a series of other causes, with their consequences, brought the Saviour to the cross, the Lamb to the slaughter. And now men are beginning to see that it is the only true preaching, — the only preaching which is to move and raise and redeem the world. And it is uttered and heard with increasing effect, not only from pulpits and in religious assemblies, but in the house and by the way, from tongue to tongue, and heart to heart, in the daily walks, the common practice, and the ordinary meetings of men. "The Lord gave the word, great was the company of preachers. Kings with their armies did flee and were discomfited." It is the voice of experiment and improvement, and the lesson of experience. Humility is showing itself stronger than pride, meekness than arrogance, peace than war, gentleness than wrath, and charity than selfishness. Ay, stronger; not only better but stronger, and stronger because better. They have not prevailed, but they are prevailing. The end of the warfare is not yet. It is probably very far off; but it is approaching. The time is approaching when Christianity shall be understood as it was preached by its author.

The completeness of the morality of the gospel, therefore, is made up of that part which has always received the approbation of men, comprising such virtues as honesty, justice, veracity, and that part which, though equally worthy of approbation, has been greatly despised and kept out of sight, comprising the self-denying, self-sacrificing, lowly, and peaceful virtues. What was once thought, and is still thought by many, to be a defective portion of the Christian code, is proving to be its distinctive strength and ornament. How faultless is that system, of which humility and gentleness were supposed to be the faults. If faultless, then endless. The foundations of Christianity, instead of being disturbed, are only settling, and consolidating, and becoming more strongly cemented than ever.

Inseparably connected with the morality of our religion, and indeed a personification of it, is the life and character of him who brought it. Some of the Christian virtues are to be deduced and enforced rather from the example of Jesus than from his direct precepts. The character of Christianity is the character of Christ. We say then, again, that there will be no end of Christianity, because there will be no end of the influence and rule of a character like that of Christ. It is the divine image. It is God manifest in the flesh. It is a form of love and majesty, full of grace and truth, which must ever be enthroned in the hearts of men, while there are good affections there to do it homage. Warm admiration, earnest gratitude, tender sympathy, unshaken loyalty, "holy hope and high humility," — all the virtues and sentiments which the Prince of Peace has called around him and appointed to honor, — form his permanent court; and before its spiritual splendor oriental magnificence grows dim. Jesus is and forever must be enthroned in the human breast. "Of his kingdom there shall be no end;" for it is a spiritual kingdom, and he himself is ever present to administer it. Centuries have no effect on the brightness of his lineaments. Purely, freshly, do love and faith behold him now, as they bow before him; and thus they ever will behold him, when marble statues are defaced, and palaces are ruins and dust.

I will mention but one more element of Christianity, inherent in its nature and inseparable from it, which gives assurance of its perpetuity. It is the doctrine, the promise, the principle of immortal life. This is brought to light in the gospel. It stands first among the glad tidings. It is clearly proclaimed; it is strongly proved. It is encumbered by no degrading superstitions. It is the high and pure sanction of a high and pure morality. It addresses itself to those hopes which are always listening for good news from the better country; to that longing after immortality which is a longing of man's nature. The news having been distinctly told, and strikingly confirmed, is it likely that it will ever be forgotten or discredited? Possessing the knowledge which they have longed for, will men ever let it go? The heavens having been opened to them, will they ask to have them shut up? Or will they close their eyes to the light which is pouring down? Having this hope, sure and steadfast, will they soon, or can they ever, relinquish it? First, they must change their nature.

I need not be told of the infidelity which is abroad. I hear it with regret, but without fear. Infidelity has always been abroad, either in disguise or openly. I know that some men will hurt themselves, and poison themselves, and throw away their best possessions, and scoff at the holiest feelings of their nature. But I also know that they cannot persuade their fellow-men to follow their example. I also know, that, while there exists among men a reverence for what is high and holy, and a hope of happiness beyond the reach of accident and death, this reverence will continue to seek the instructions, and this hope to accept the promises and rest on the proofs, of the gospel of Christ; and this will be so, notwithstanding some unfortunate persons have divested themselves of reverence and cast away hope. Go and ask the son or the daughter where the parent is who nursed their helpless infancy, and sung to their childhood amidst its sunshines and showers, and loved, counselled, suffered, and still forgave; ask them where that parent is, now that the face of father or mother is seen no more. They will say, In heaven! Ask the parents where that child is whom they so lately held and led by the hand, listening to its fresh wonder, cheered by its cheerfulness, and taught by its questionings and its purity. They may not be able to speak, but they will look upwards, and their hearts will answer, In heaven! There they have placed its image; there they see it smiling brightly upon them, in the labors of the day and in the silent watches of the night; and all the hundred hands of impiety and unbelief cannot tear it down. Nor can they take from the weary pilgrim the hope of his rest, from the traveller the sight of his home, from the virtuous and the lovers of virtue the prospect of a better world.

In such foundations as these the structure of our religion is laid; and they are as firm as the everlasting hills, and firmer. All this faith and hope in God, in virtue, in Christ, in heaven; all this love of what is greatest and most worthy, is not to be exchanged on a sudden for what is nothing at best. When I fear for Christianity, it will be after I have despaired of everything spiritual and everything good. When I behold the beauty of the light, and the fitness of the eye to receive and rejoice in it, I no more fear that the Sun of Righteousness will set in shadows, than that the burning centre of our planetary system will fall from the skies.

"He shall reign over the house of Jacob forever, and of his kingdom there shall be no end." Other kingdoms shall change and perish; other governments shall be destroyed; the old sound of crushing thrones has not ceased; they have been falling in our own times all around us, and others will fall in the times that are coming after us. The kingdom of Christ is not dependent upon them, and will not fall with them. Nor will it pass away, though some of the forms and institutions which men have connected with it should be laid aside. These things are not the substance of Christianity, and Christianity cannot be disturbed by their alteration. He who considers the foundations of the Messiah's kingdom, will see that they do not consist in these things, but are the same with the foundations of the eternal throne. "Thy throne, O God, is forever and ever; the sceptre of thy kingdom is a right sceptre."

December 25, 1832.

SERMON XV.

INDEPENDENCE ON HUMAN SYMPATHY.

And yet I am not alone, because the Father is with me.—
John xvi. 32.

No sublimer moral spectacle can be presented to the sight of men than that of one who, though he should be deprived of all the usual supports of friendship and sympathy, yet falls not, because he is spiritually upheld; of one who, though in the path of duty he be deserted by all visible companions, yet stops not, falters not, because he is then brought into closer communion with the Almighty Spirit and All-sufficient Friend; of one who, when left alone, is yet not alone, and complains not of defection and loneliness, because One, whom he knows to be his Father, is with him. Such a spectacle is brought before us by the words of the text.

Jesus was not insensible to human sympathies. He loved all mankind, and he sought their love. He loved his disciples, and loved them unto the end. The end was now just at hand; and his whole parting discourse to them and prayer for them prove how tenderly he loved them. Of all who had ever followed him, these eleven only remained, on that night when he was betrayed; and he foresaw that their allegiance would not stand the last trial, but that they would forsake him in the impending hour of darkness. "Behold the hour cometh, yea, is now come, that ye shall be scattered, every man to his own, and shall leave me alone." Think you that Jesus was indifferent to the failure of those friends whom he had chosen out of the whole world? He was not indifferent to it; he felt it keenly; it contributed to the bitterness of the cup which he was about to drain; but he could not permit it to overcome him; he was sustained by higher sympathies; he felt the presence of a holier power. "And yet I am not alone, because the Father is with me."

I would inculcate from this passage a due independence on human sympathy; not a disregard of it, but an independence on it, a power of doing without it; a power which must exist within us, and must come down, with every other good and perfect gift, from above. It is impossible that we should disregard this sympathy of our fellow-men. It would not be well that we should. The desire of it is one of the primary wants of our being. The comfort and happiness to be derived from it are inestimable. But still we must learn to do without it. We must so train and discipline ourselves, that, if it should fail us, if it should be withdrawn from us, we may not droop and mourn as utterly forlorn and helpless, but gather up our own strength and go forward, trusting in that strength, because it is given us from God.

We must learn to be superior to the need of human sympathy, for this very reason, that if we do not, occasions and seasons will come when the support of that sympathy will be refused to us, and when we shall consequently be left alone, wholly alone, and shall fall. This is not mere supposition or remote probability. Hardly a life, among the vast number of human lives, is without such occasions and seasons. They occur to our experience and observation continually, and they occur in great variety.

You have an end in view, an important moral end. You see it clearly, and you tell your vision. You apprehend the means which are requisite to accomplish or promote that end, and you propose those means to the favor and adoption of other men. But the end which you see so clearly, they do not see at all; or, if they see it, they do not see its importance.

The means which you propose call for too much exertion, or for some personal sacrifice which they are not disposed to make, even if they see your end, and acknowledge in some degree its importance. Your views are not embraced. Your efforts are not seconded. You meet with no sympathy. Do you feel alone? Do you experience within yourself the heart-sinkings of a deserted and desolate man? In a measure and for a time you do. You cannot help feeling so. You are constituted to feel so. But if you have foreseen this disappointment as possible, and have guarded yourself against its effects; if you have accustomed yourself to a spiritual independence and solitude, you will not give up that end, you will pursue it with such aid as you can obtain, and as far as possible without aid. You will be sensible of internal aid and companionship; and with that strength you will bear up against averted looks, against cold words, against sneers and ridicule, against the despondent pleadings of your own solitary affections; and you will persevere, longing for human sympathy, and yet able to go on, and determined to go on, without it.

Again; a subject interests your feelings as you have no reason or right to expect it can interest the feelings of other men. They do not sympathize with you, simply because they cannot sympathize with you. The subject is one which is brought before you, or which is connected with you in a manner which naturally gives it a charm or a value, or, on the other hand, a pain or discomfort, with which others are not affected. What will you do? You want the sympathy of your neighbors. But you cannot force their sympathy. Sympathy is not controlled by the laws of force. It must be yielded spontaneously, or not at all. From the circumstances of the case, it cannot now be yielded spontaneously, because your neighbors cannot feel as you feel, and therefore you cannot have it. What will you do? Will you complain? Then you will make yourself more unhappy than before, and without accomplishing your desire. Will you assume an indifference yourself toward the subject which excites you and does not excite others? This perhaps you ought not to do, even if you can; or perhaps cannot do, at any rate, on account of your inevitable relations with it. You must stand in your own strength, and stand alone. You must be content to superintend and guide your own feelings, and enjoy or suffer them without communication, because you cannot reasonably demand that others should share them.

Suppose, again, that the sympathy of others ought to be given you, and yet is not, through their fault, their obtuseness, their frivolity, or their cruelty. Here there is blame attaching to them, but the same duty and necessity of independence incumbent upon you. Your duty plainly is, not to despair because there is a want of proper feeling in the world, or in your neighborhood, but to maintain yourself on your own sense of right, and your own individual relations, trusts, and responsibilities. Whether your neighbors are right or wrong, whether their conduct in respect to you is justifiable or unjustifiable, one thing is certain, that they do not join you, that they do not go along with you, that they leave you alone. It is yours to determine whether this solitude is to be supplied, and how.

Suppose another case, and one which is not uncommon. You have suffered some loss, some great loss. The burden of your grief is heavy upon you. You seek to have it alleviated. Your situation calls for sympathy, and you receive sympathy. But you do not receive so much as you require, so much as you suppose to be your due, so much as your excitement craves. You find that the sympathy expressed is unsatisfying; consoles you not; supports you not; leaves you still in a manner alone. This is not always because there is a want of a good disposition to console you to the utmost, but sometimes because your friends lack the ability to put their sympathy into the most effective and consoling form, and sometimes because any form of sympathy must appear tame to your excited sensibilities, must feel cold to your warmly bleeding heart. Accuse not your friends of apathy. Charge them not with want of feeling. If they do not possess feeling, your accusations will not give it to them. If they do possess it, your reproaches will add to their unhappiness, without alleviating your own. How can they feel as much as you do yourself? And even if they should feel as much, or even more, and should express their feeling in the strongest and best chosen terms, neither their words nor their tears could restore to you what you had lost, or fill up the void in your bosom. Human sympathy of the most perfect character has a limited operation. It cannot do everything. Bless it for what it does, and demand not of it impossibilities or miracles. Bring your mind to the conclusion, that there are woes which it cannot fully relieve; burdens which it cannot lift away from off your spirit; occasions when it must leave you comparatively alone, and when you must be made aware of its insufficiency, and aware of the need of something else, something mightier, something holier, for support and consolation.

Another reason which may be proposed for

the cultivation of independence on human sympathy is its intrinsic dignity and propriety, which are so manifest that they always command respect, and win a favor at last which is denied to a weak and importunate dependence. What is the consequence of a person's continually and beseechingly throwing himself upon the sympathies even of his friends? He wears out those sympathies. They cannot supply his incessant demands. They grow weary in the thankless task of bearing or endeavoring to bear the troubles of one who does little or nothing to bear his own troubles. There is an aspect of mendicancy in his conduct, which is felt to be troublesome, and which rather repels than secures the best regards of friendship and offices of charity. Whereas a person who is careful not to intrude his sorrows on the attention of others is respected for his manliness, and loved for his good sense and forbearance; and fully gains the sympathy for which he does not beg. Sympathies flow in upon such a man, in free tides, from all affectionate hearts. Sooner or later they will flow in upon him. If there are no walls of prejudice about him, to check their access, they will flow in at once; but in spite of all obstacles they will reach him at last; they will reach and surround the man who has shown that he has deserved them, and that he can, when they are withheld or refused, live and be refreshed and sustained without them. It is an unquestionable fact, that the most generous and ample sympathy rendered by man is not rendered till the object of it has proved himself to be superior to it; not coldly or arrogantly superior to it, but so fortified, so maintained by an inward might, that he is no needy dependent upon it. One powerful consideration, therefore, for the cultivation of independence on human sympathy is, that the best sympathy is finally given to independence. A bright example of this truth is the once deserted Saviour. What a crowd of sympathies, what a countless pilgrimage of affections, now flock about him, on that loneliest spot in his whole life, where he was betrayed, denied, and forsaken of men. All the sympathy which has been rendered to all the greatest and wisest of our race, is not to be mentioned in comparison with that unreckoned and inconceivable amount which goes forth from age to age, and hangs round the image of the despised and crucified;— of him, who, in the Garden of Gethsemane, in the Hall of Pilate, on the Mount of Calvary, was left alone, and yet was not alone, because the Father was with him.

Do you ask how this independence, so indispensable, so honorable, is to be acquired? I refer you again to that example. I refer you to the words of the text. Jesus, though left alone, was not alone, because the Father was with him. He did not sink in the time of his desertion, because he was upheld of God. He could spare the company, and pardon the defection of his disciples, because he could resort to the all-sufficient source of love and light and mercy.

Where he resorted, we must also resort; and where he found strength, there must we find it also, for it is to be found nowhere else. When I have spoken of internal strength, I have intended no strength which belongs to a man's own nature, and originates in his own self; for I do not believe in the sufficiency of any such strength for the trying emergencies of his condition.

> "Man's wisdom is to seek
> His strength in God alone;
> An angel even would be weak,
> Who trusted in his own."

There is a proud and hard self-confidence, which will, to outward appearance, bear a man up through much tribulation and desolatences. But there is no comfort, no relief, no refreshment, in such endurance and struggling. The real and consoling strength can only come from above; can only be given from God; can only be imparted by the conviction that God is present, that God hears, sees, pities, and will reward. The want of human sympathy is only to be supplied by communion with the Holy and Eternal Spirit. The defects, the insufficiency of human sympathy, are only to be remedied by an abiding and religious sense of the fulness and perfection of that love and care with which an Almighty Father watches over his children. You can never feel isolated or deserted, if you have accustomed yourself to heavenly companionship. Whatever your sorrows, whatever your loneliness may be, in whatever way you may be disappointed or forsaken, a practical faith that the mightiest of all beings, that the wisest and best of all beings, is ever near you, fills up the void, and surrounds you with an eternal sympathy.

> " Who is alone, if God be nigh?
>   Who shall repine at loss of friends,
> While he has One of boundless power,
>   Whose constant kindness never ends;
> Whose presence felt enhances joy,
>   Whose love can stop the flowing tear,
> And cause upon the darkest cloud
>   The pledge of mercy to appear?"

Withdraw not from men; but draw nearer and more near every day unto God. Repel not human sympathies; slight not the expressions of human kindness, however imperfect and inadequate they may be; break not with rudeness a single tie, though it have no more substance and strength than a gossamer thread, which connects you with your brethren: but cultivate, above and before all, those sentiments of piety which render the presence of God a reality to your spirit, and make him your Father and your Friend. Then you will not complain of the want of human sympathy, for you will be possessed of a love which is infinitely better. Then you will not be hurt by the seeming chilliness and insufficiency of that sympathy, because you will be convinced that everything human must be imperfect, and because you will be satisfied with the sufficiency of God. Then you will have communion and sympathy with Jesus Christ, who loved all men most deeply at that very hour when he was forsaken of all men, and who, when forsaken and alone, yet was not alone, because the Father was with him.

June 5, 1836.

SERMON XVI.

CHRIST OUR FELLOW-SUFFERER.

O my Father, if it be possible, let this cup pass from me. — *Matt.* xxvi. 39.

To some most serious Christians, the passage which I have announced as my text has seemed big with difficulty. They are accustomed to view all the words and actions of Jesus through the medium of a preconceived metaphysical theory or system, by which he is indeed mistily and vaguely magnified to their imaginations, but rendered distant to their understandings, and uncertain to their hearts. It has militated with their apprehensions of the nature and dignity of the Saviour, that he should sue to escape from suffering; that, when the figure of the cross was presented to him, distinct and near, he should pray that a door might be opened through which he might flee from it; that, when the cup of a bitter death was held close to his lips, he should supplicate his Father that it might be withdrawn from them. Here is the difficulty, — that one of eternal dignity should be afraid of pain and death; and much has been said and invented to explain the scriptural statement.

But there is no difficulty in this portion of our Lord's history, if we will set our theories aside, and read it with our sincere and natural affections. Then we shall find that it is consistent, worthy, and true as it stands, without explanation or apology. Then we shall find that there is nothing in it incompatible with the proper dignity of the Saviour, or with that temper of devout and filial submission which was so leading a feature of his character. We shall find that it is full of harmony and full of instruction.

Let us consider the passage as it is simply presented to us. If I read it with my heart open, I perceive how naturally the ejaculation broke from our Saviour's lips, under the circumstances in which he was placed, the crisis in his mission to which he had come; and it so touches me, so addresses itself, as it rises to heaven, to corresponding emotions within me, that I bless the evangelist for having recorded it. My own human nature owns a sympathy in it, and derives a support from it, which it could not have owned in any exhibition of indifference to suffering, and could not have derived from any words of excited heroism. Alone, the dark hour advancing, his friends sleeping, his enemies watching, seizure and torture at hand, his brow presses the damp soil of the garden, and the midnight silence is broken by his earnest prayer, " O my Father, if it be possible, let this cup pass from me!" This is nature and this is truth. I ask not whether it accords with a divine nature, or with an angelic nature; I feel that it accords with *my* nature, and enters into communion with my nature, and is of much more service to my spirit than anything stoical or foreign from my nature could have been. I feel that even the feebleness of my nature, in its seasons of oppression and sorrow, is spoken to and sympathetically comforted by these imploring words of my Lord. Here is a perfect nature, speaking precisely as my own nature would be impelled to utter itself in prospect of great trial; and by this fellowship I am assured and soothed, and am taught that my feebleness, or what may be termed so, is not sinful, but, being implanted by the Author of my nature, has its good ends and its saving purposes. It was, indeed, through suffering, felt as it is felt by ourselves, that the perfection of our Saviour's nature received its holiest crown; according to the Scripture which assures us that he " was made perfect through suffering." And it is probably in reference to this very scene of his agony in the Garden of Gethsemane, that the author of the Epistle to the Hebrews speaks, when he says of him, " Who in the days of his flesh, when he had offered up prayers and supplications with strong crying and tears unto him that was able to save him from death, and was heard in that he feared ; though he were a Son, yet learned he obedience by the things which he suffered; and being made perfect, he became the author of eternal salvation unto all them that obey him."

Jesus did not court death nor choose pain. He makes no boast, sends forth no challenge. How different is this simplicity from the deportment of some of his followers in circumstances of extremity, who have gone beyond their master, and plunged into extravagance and fanaticism. Compare these words of his with the words of some of those martyrs who suffered in his cause. His deprecate agony; theirs invite it. They have rushed to the cross or the stake with a mad joy; they have even sported with their awful situation in wild words of jest. Place their reported sayings by the side of his supplication in Gethsemane, and judge whether the former resemble the latter, or are countenanced by it. I say not that all Christ's faithful witnesses have in this manner exceeded. I reverence the noble army of martyrs, many of whom have confessed and suffered as became their cause in all things. Nor do I mean to say that there is no nature and not a dash of truth in the enthusiastic bearing and expressions of those who have smiled at death and saluted him; for I charge not even these with hypocrisy. But the nature which they have exhibited is an excited, goaded, intoxicated nature; and if they have been true to nature, they have been true to the pride of nature and to its capacity of high excitation. They have thus shown me, indeed, that there is something lofty even in the errors of my nature, when the original impulse is given by a good cause. But they have afforded me no proper example. How could they, when their example has deviated so far from that of our common Lord? They have offered me no enduring sympathy and no steady support; for I can hold no enduring sympathy with a fitful outbreak of zeal and daring, which my composed mind cannot approve, and to which my own nature may not at any time be equal; and I can derive no steady support from declarations which have been prompted by doubtful motives, by earth-born passion as largely as by heaven-born faith.

And when I search to the bottom of this matter, I arrive at the conclusion that no well-balanced, unexaggerated, human nature or being can ever despise, or be indifferent to, loss, shame, pain, and death; that is, can ever despise or be indifferent to them absolutely and unconditionally. It can be so sustained as to rise superior to them, and it may prefer them, vastly prefer them as alternatives; but it must always avoid them for their own single sakes, it must always escape from them if it can, if it can consistently with honor, self-respect, obedience to principle and to God. That which is bitter is bitter, and can only be sweetened to the imagination by being compared with something which is more bitter, or by being presented as the only means of attaining that which is sweet and good and essentially desirable. Suffering is suffering; and you cannot teach human nature to be indifferent to it, because he who made it has made it susceptible of suffering. And here it is that I feel the value of my Saviour's prayer. Jesus sympathizes with me when I shrink from the prospect of pain; for there was an hour when he shrunk from it himself, and, in extreme distress, begged to be delivered from it, if it were possible. There was no show of bravery in him, when the sweat dropped from him like blood, and he cried amidst the gloom of that last night, cried out that the cup might be taken away; and this assures me, that no show of bravery is required of me in the hour of my distress, and that I am guilty of no improper weakness, and prefer no undutiful petition, when I am subdued and melted, and pray that the dreaded pangs may be spared me. I find him near to me in the valley of tears and sorrows, not rebuking me, but sanctifying my sad appeals, and permitting me to borrow his own words in making my petition. I love him for his simple, undisguised, unmingled truth; I love him for taking on himself my nature so entirely; for not only teaching me and arming me, but weeping with me and even fearing with me. And loving him in this wise, and comforted by his sympathy when I weep and fear, I am better prepared to follow and imitate him when he submits, endures, and triumphs. Reassured in my trembling and yet importunate griefs, by hearing him exclaim, " O my Father, if it be possible, let this cup pass from me," I am the more ready to pursue his prayer, and add, " Nevertheless, not as I will, but as thou wilt."

My friends, we are continually praying, all of us, that the cup may pass from us. He who fears that illness may break up his cherished plans, and cast a lasting shadow over his temporal prospects; he who fears that the fluctuating elements, or the fickle times, or the more fickle purposes of men, may reduce him and his family to narrow and dependent poverty; he who fears that the confidence which he has reposed is misplaced and abused, and that one whom he had called friend will betray him; he who fears that death has come upon him unawares and prematurely, to snatch him away from all his hopes and labors, and from those who love him and look to him with intense observance; all they who fear that they may be presently called to abide some great agony of flesh or spirit, will pray in agony that, if it be possible, the cup may pass from them. And who will forbid or check the prayer? Not the Author and Finisher of our faith; not he who prayed with his face on the ground in Gethsemane; not Jesus.

The once blooming and light-hearted child is lying pale on its little bed. To the anxious questioning of its parents the physician has returned a grave and dubious reply. They look on its face with a feeling which never shot through their hearts till now, and with all the earnestness of him who prayed in the garden, they pray that the dear blossom may be spared to them. O Father! if it be possible, if it be possible, let this cup pass from us! We would hold the child thou hast given us yet longer in our arms; we would warm him yet longer in our bosoms; we would listen to his voice, watch over his opening intellect, nurse him into maturity, lead him into life! O Father, if it be possible! Who will interrupt them in their prayer? who will chide them for it? Not Jesus.

A friend has been by our side through many a varied year, participating with us in every care, helping us to bear every burden, rejoicing in our joy, and wounded by our sorrow. As he is still engaged in kindly offices, his countenance becomes altered, and shows that the summons is issued for his removal, and that the might of the last hours is upon him. The past rises before us, bringing looks, words, and deeds of affection and devotedness, and we can hardly support the thought that these are never more to be repeated, but now there is to be an end of all. Our reason and our religion will acknowledge that the separation is wisely ordered by him who holds our times in his hand, but our human nature will first cry out, "O my Father, if it be possible, let this cup pass from me!" And who will arrest the cry? Not Jesus.

Surely, it is among the greatest of our privileges, that, in seasons of mortal weakness, we have the sympathy of him who was strong to conquer death and the grave; that, when the cup of disappointment, or bereavement, or sudden fear, is brought to our lips, and we pray to have it removed, we may be conscious of the sympathy of the well beloved Son, who prayed that the cup might also pass from him. But if we would experience all the advantage of our Saviour's sympathy, let us proceed and finish his prayer. Let us add, with a resignation as humble as our pleading was fervent, "Nevertheless, not as we will, but as thou wilt." If it be not the will of God that our request, whatever it may be, and however urgent we may be in offering it, should be granted, then it is impossible, and it is our part to submit. If it be not his will to comply with our desires, it is not best that they should be complied with; it is neither for our good nor for the good of others; in fine, it is not right; and therefore our submission should be sincere, and even cheerful, though our prayer was importunate and sorrowful. If we would pray with Jesus, we must pray with the same temper of final and complete resignation which animated his prayer, with the same deep conviction that the will of our Father is eternal justice, and infinite wisdom, and infinite mercy, and therefore not only must, but ought to be done. After we have prayed to be spared, and are shown in the event that we cannot be, then it becomes us to drain the cup as he did, with patience and fortitude and charity like his. Thus and thus only are we to enter fully into his sympathies. He prayed in Gethsemane that the cup of suffering and death might pass from him; and thrice he prayed so; but each time he also prayed that his Father's will might be done; and when he came to Calvary, and the cup was held to him, did he not drink it? Who ever suffered with equal constancy, with equal dignity? Nor did he at any intervening time endeavor to escape from pain or death by any means which were inconsistent with truth, love, obedience, and duty. This was to him impossible; and it should be so to us.

We learn, then, from this part of our Saviour's example, how truly and entirely the tenderest susceptibility to pain, and the most intense desire to be saved from it, may consist with the holiest resignation and the firmest courage and fortitude. We learn that, though our nature may be shaken to its foundations, our virtuous principles must not yield a hair; that no prospect of suffering is to move us from the right; that no presence of suffering is to overcome our faith, our duty, our piety. We are not called to disguise the apprehensions and quailings of our nature; for Jesus did not disguise his; but in the same simplicity, the same directness of spirit, we are to dare, in the path of evident duty and God's commandment, we are to dare and endure all to the end.

And having learned, in much tribulation and by solemn experience, the great value of our Saviour's sympathy, it will become us to hold our spirits in readiness to go forth and meet him at all times; to sympathise with him who has so effectually sympathized with us; to serve him who has liberated and saved us. In many ways this sympathy is to be manifested: by the faithful deference which appeals to his decisions, and is satisfied with them and thankful for them; by the susceptibility which is alive to the abuses of his name and the perversions of his cause; by the dutiful observance which enters into his mind, and adopts his views, and looks on mankind with those same eyes of earnest and unaffected benevolence. He is not worthy to resort to the sympathy of Jesus, who rudely questions his instructions, coarsely discusses his claims, and, most irreverently reversing the relation between them, calls into judgment his Judge. He is not worthy to resort to the sympathy of Jesus, who is careless whether men believe in him and obey him, or not; who feels no emotion when his name, at which every knee should bow, is mentioned with slight or dishonor; who is indifferent to the advancement of his cause and spread of his religion. And especially is he not worthy to resort to that blessed sympathy, who is not melted at the thought, that it was for him that Christ wept, prayed, and suffered, and does not faithfully resolve that his sins shall not crucify the Lord afresh, and that he will live his true disciple, in repentance and a holy life. By humility, by affectionate reverence, by hearty service, by love unfeigned, do we enter into the mind and heart of the Saviour, and render back to him our sympathy, in free though poor return for his. Then may we go to him at all times, by the path of this admitted communion, in times of depression, of fear, of anguish, and we shall surely be received and comforted.

November 5, 1837.

SERMON XVII.

SEEING THE DEPARTED.

A little while, and ye shall not see me; and again a little while, and ye shall see me, because I go to the Father.—John xvi. 16.

No wonder that the disciples were perplexed by these asseverations of their Master, and could not tell what he said. His going away from them through the gate of death, before he had manifested himself to the world after their ideas of the Messiah's glory, was an event which hardly any form of words could make them realize. How it was that in a little while they should not see him, not see him at the very period when they looked to see him in the true light of his triumphant splendor; and again how it was that when they did see him, it should be because he went to his Father, they could not comprehend.

The explanation came with the death, resurrection, and ascension of their Lord. When they had received the Spirit, and had become spiritual, then they perceived the actual and spiritual sense of these words, and of others which had been equally unintelligible to them before. A little while only after he was thus tenderly conversing with them, his form and countenance were disfigured by base and cruel usage, he was crucified most ignominiously, he was laid in the tomb, and hid from the sight of his disciples. They saw him not. The light of hope and of his presence were equally extinct. The fires of pride and ambition were put out. They were left in darkness. He, in whom they had trusted as the Redeemer of Israel, had been taken away before he had, in their view, even commenced the work of redemption. It was as if they had been suddenly struck blind. Night was upon their senses, and dismay and confusion in their hearts, concealing from them the way of Jesus. He was dead, and they did not see him.

But again a little while, at the end of three days only, and they did see him, in the midst of them, as before, and more clearly, more truly than before. And though he again left them at his ascension, they still saw him, because he went to his Father. From that time forth they always saw him, with the distinct vision of faith, at the right hand of God. They never lost sight of him more. They are with him, and they see him now.

The above cited passage of gospel history has led me to the consideration of the two following topics: the sudden disappearance of our best blessings to the eye of sense, and their perpetuity and immortality in the sight of faith and religion.

"What is this that he saith, A little while? we cannot tell what he saith." Thus whispers the unenlightened, unrenewed human heart. A little while! Is it for a little while that these joys, these gifts, these friends, my pleasant time, my smiling fortune, the wisdom which leads me, the careful love which provides for me, the innocence which delights me, the sympathy which constantly, though almost imperceptibly, warms and cheers me, even as the patient sun ripens the fruit, — is it for a little while only that these are to be mine? I see no marks of decay, no symptoms of disease, no indications of vanishing, among them. I look for their increase, for their maturity, not their blight, not their destruction. What is this that the monitor, the preacher saith, A little while? Oh no! it is for a long, long while, surely, that I shall keep and enjoy them.

And then comes the shadow, the blight, the departure. The blessing disappears suddenly; suddenly to us, because we thought it was to stay indefinitely with us. However long we had possessed it, we feel that it was only for a little while. Days shrink into minutes, and years into hours. O that while we had it, we had valued it more, improved it more. But now it is vanished, and we see it not. It appears not to our eyes among the providences of God. It was, and quickly it was not. That is all. Friends go away, and we are slow to ask whither they are gone; but sorrow fills our hearts, because they go so unexpectedly and so soon, and because we do not see them. We are unprepared to lose them, and we feel and speak as if we had really lost them. It had never been promised us that we should retain them for any length of time. A little while, a little while only, is the allotted duration of that which is mortal, and the warning of this truth is fairly written and proclaimed, and perpetually repeated. Did we ever see any sublunary enjoyment last so long as to appear longer than a little while to him who held it? Do not young children fall from the tree of life like blossoms? Youths and maidens, do they not one year stand among us crowned with bloom and freshness as with flowers, and the next, are not the only flowers near them those which are growing on their graves? And yet we are unprepared. There is a voice, as explicit as the words of Jesus to his disciples, constantly telling us, A little while, and ye shall not see the delight of your eyes, — but we understand it and credit it with no more readiness than they did; and when the saying is fulfilled, we are as much disappointed and disturbed as they were; and while we are thus disappointed, while earthly hopes and thoughts, fears and regrets alone, are in our hearts, we do not see the lost objects of our love. They are gone; not merely gone to another place, but gone entirely away, vanished, perished. We no longer see them among existing things; and if Christian faith comes not into our hearts with its mist-dispelling light, we never see them more.

But it is one of God's purposes in taking them away, that we shall see them again, and in truer and more satisfying aspects than before. "Again a little while, and ye shall see me, because I go to the Father." God would have us know that nothing truly lives, but that which lives with him, and to him. The most effectual teacher of this knowledge is death. Death compels us to look somewhere for consolation, and we perceive that it is only to be found in religion. The loss of what is transitory leads us to an acquaintance with that which is enduring. In a little while, we learn how vain it was to have calculated on the abiding of that which must go away; or to be surprised or offended at the quick departure of that which had told us that it was going soon. Life spreads out before us far beyond the earthly confines within which we had bounded it, and ends only in God the Father, in whom it first began. And then we see that all our times are and ever shall be in his hand. Then our blessings reappear, each one surrounded with a glory. In a little while the graves open, and the buried ones rise up, clothed with white and shining garments; and they are now always in our sight, because they are with their Father and our Father.

There is a sense, indeed, in which we see the departed without the intervention of religion and the enlightening process of faith. It is an act of memory which brings them before us in both our sleeping and waking hours, and the tenacity of affection which will not suffer their images to fade. We dream of them in the watches of the night; and every place of their former presence, as we see it by the light of day, restores to us their presence again. But these visions, though there is a soothing, or, at least, a softening influence proceeding from them, are deeply melancholy in their main effect upon the mind, when not introduced and quickened by the faith which shows them in the care of the Father of spirits. They are shades only, thin and flitting shades; and their "airy tongues" can say no more than that those whose forms they are, are lost forever. There is something very touching to the human affections, so touching that it has been copied and recopied, and engraved upon mourning seals, in the thought which has supposed a voice asking among grass-grown tombs, "Where are they?"—and an echo from those tombs returning for answer the single word, "Where!" It is very touching, because it is so very sad; for no one will say that there is any consolation in it, or any Christianity. It is the wailing of a tender, and yet a blind and groping, a dark and faithless heart. He who possesses the Christian hope, full of immortality, he who has perhaps gained that hope in the midst of sorrow and through the instrumentality, of death, will, in the same situation, forbear to arouse by a desponding question a desponding echo; but he will look up, and say, A little while, and I did not see them, and again a little while, and I did see them, and I always see them, because they have gone to their Father.

Such a vision is not a vision of empty shades, but of living souls, of living souls receiving continually new streams of life from the living God; and not only life, but holiness, which is the better life of heaven. Are we not all, all who see those who are gone to the Father, sensible that there is an added beauty to the countenances, and an added excellence to the characters of those whom we thus see? And this is, I am persuaded, not merely the fond suggestion of partiality, but an admonition of the very truth, a reflection of heavenly light upon their forms. Are they not better, purer, wiser than before, being now so near the Fountain? Having gone to their Father, are they not holier than they could have been with us? In his presence are not the virtuous sinless, the just made perfect, and the pious sainted? We see then the reality, when we see a glory round them brighter than they wore on earth. The friend or relative who had on earth a few faults, and yet as few, perhaps, as mortal ever had, is now to the religious eye of our observant spirit without fault; and we are not deceived, for it is really so. The child whom we regarded with tender, sometimes even with compassionate love, as we gazed upon it in its innocence and helplessness, we still see as a child, after it has left a world in which it stayed a little while. Its features, its stature, and its voice are still those of infancy, for we can only see it in these respects as it was when it went away. But is not our love now mingled with somewhat of reverence, a reverence different from that which we feel for purity alone, and such as we cannot feel for a child on earth? And is there not deep truth also in this sentiment, when we consider that the child is gone from its parents on earth, and lives with its Father in heaven?

It appears to me, that he who, without forgetting the duties which are required of him in his several relations here, yet lives, as a Christian should live, more and more in a spiritual world, and sees the worthy ones who have departed, because they have gone to their Father, must feel richer in his spirit within him as, to outward appearance, he loses more. There is a period of mortal life at which the friends who are gone begin to bear a large proportion to those who remain, if they do not even outnumber them. The Christian man beholds the heavenly company increase of those who wait for him. He finds himself living more in the past and less in the future time of his earthly life. He loses not his cheerfulness, but he is continually acquiring thoughtfulness. The bonds between heaven and him are multiplying. His faithful eye beholds, and his faithful heart records the lengthening train of the departed. And not only his nearest relatives and most intimate friends are on the register of his spirit, but those whose sweetness and worth he has known from the communion of a few years or months, or even from a few casual meetings, are all added to the list as they put on immortality. Of these he thinks, and with these he converses, with increasing frequency, and with a pleasure which the unbelieving and the doubting cannot experience. As he lives on, the number of his earthly companions is every year decreasing, till perhaps they all go, and then what is there for him but to wait? He will not grieve, but wait and hope. The departed are not a source of sorrow, but now his only solace and joy. In the cheerful words of an old poet, he may say,

> "They all are gone into a world of light,
> And I alone sit lingering here;
> Their very memory is fair and bright,
> And my sad thoughts doth clear."

You perceive that this vision is necessarily and only the vision of a Christian faith and hope. The holy dead are seen, actually seen as real existences, because they go to the Father of our Lord Jesus Christ. Every son and daughter of God, sent here for a little while, and saved from wandering, returns home to the Father. There they dwell, and there the faith which is confirmed in Christ will clearly see them.

And the Captain of their salvation, the first-born from the dead, through whom we have this sight, shall not he also be seen by his disciples? Shall we not see the great friend by whom the souls of our friends are seen? It must be a strange and a cold faith which sees him not, which does not love to see him, and earnestly and affectionately to contemplate him. He should be viewed not only as the Teacher on earth, but as the Lord in heaven. He was on earth but a little while. He is risen, ascended, gone to his Father; and there he continues his offices of supervision, and help, and mercy, and can never resign them till all is subdued. I am aware of nothing in any creed professedly Christian, — I am sure there is nothing in mine, — which forbids us to see our Lord as present and glorified, or to draw near to him in the solemn exercises of the spirit, or to lift up our hearts to him, if not in prayer as to the Supreme, yet in love and praise and earnest ejaculation, as to the well beloved and highly exalted Son, the Head of the Church below as of the Church above, through whom we have access to the Father, and who ever intercedes with the Father for us. And the vision of those departed saints who live with God can be only a full, and satisfying, and Christian vision when it presents them as fed by the Lamb who is in the midst of the throne, and led by him "unto living fountains of waters."

May 5, 1833.

SERMON XVIII.

THE CROWN OF THORNS.

And when they had platted a crown of thorns, they put it upon his head, and a reed in his right hand; and they bowed the knee before him, and mocked him, saying, Hail, King of the Jews! — *Matt.* xxvii. 29.

NEVER but once did he whose kingdom was of heaven and of the spirit appear with the outward insignia of royalty; and then they were forced upon him in mockery. Never but once did the Prince of Peace hold a visible sceptre in his hand; and then it was a reed, with which his scoffing subjects smote him. Never but once did the King of Israel wear an earthly crown; and then it was a crown of thorns, to pierce his sacred temples, and first shed that innocent and precious blood which soon was to flow more copiously on the ignominious tree.

Our sympathies are strongly interested in this scene; and our feelings of compassion for the insulted sufferer, and of indignation against the vile herd who so pitilessly abused him, are aroused within us. And so they ought to be. We should be unworthy of the name of Christians, and even of men, could we contemplate the bruised and wounded person of our outraged Master without being deeply moved; could we see merit thus rejected, holiness thus violated, the purest and most disinterested benevolence thus shamefully rewarded, and the serenest glory thus deridingly and painfully crowned, without having all the generous passions of our nature excited in behalf of the meek and unresisting victim.

But let us quiet these passions now, and put them to rest. Let the soul separate itself for a while from them, and in calm abstraction regard this scene, with all its spiritual and moral associations, and then it will be seen to be a fitting coronation. Yes; that very crown of thorns, its points gilded with that sacred blood, will prove to be, apart from the cruelty, injustice, and ingratitude which placed it there, the most fitting circle for the brows of Jesus of Nazareth, the King of the Jews.

What other crown would we wish to see there? Among all the wreaths and diadems which have been fashioned by human love, admiration, or servility, or assumed by human pride or power, which would we select as worthy to be bound on the Messiah's head?

We have heard of crowns of flowers, worn on occasions of joy and festivity. Shall we cull one of these? O leave them on the heads of the gay and thoughtless. Leave them to bloom and breathe and wither. Such poor, frail things would ill become the forehead of the King of Righteousness. We will not join with his enemies, and mock him too. We will not mock the Man of Sorrows with a chaplet of flowers. It is true that he did not come to forbid social pleasures, or to frown away one harmless delight from the abodes of men. But it is also true that he came to restrain excess; to denounce slothful indulgence and voluptuousness; to incite men to serious usefulness and duty, to moral diligence and watchfulness; to refine and exalt their pleasures, by redeeming them from the bondage of sense, and uniting them with heavenly hope and holy love; to give reality and satisfactoriness to their joys, by resting them on secure foundations, and making them innocent, spiritual, and thoughtful. This was an essential part of his mission. In performing it, who can say that he sought pleasure, as men are apt to count pleasure? Who can say that his life was one of ease, that his pathway ran through flowers? The rough desert saw his temptation and his victory; the sad mountains knew his footsteps, and listened silently to his prayers. The devoted city and the grave of his friend bore witness to his tears. His whole life was a toil and a contest. From his very birth, which was in a manger, his blood was thirsted for by jealous royalty. Before his ministry began, he labored in an humble occupation, subjected to his parents. While his ministry continued, he was constantly going about doing good, resisting evil, and making himself acquainted with grief, disease, and death in all their forms; while they, in all their forms, heard his voice and obeyed it. Often was he driven from places whither he had borne, and wherein he would have dispensed, the salvation of God. He had not where to lay his head. How could the crown of pleasure suit it at all? It was lifted up fearlessly amid the tumults of the populace, fearlessly in the presence of the rich and great. It has just been bowed in meek submission to drink the cup of agony which his Father had given him to drink. It is now raised in calm and enduring dignity, pale and bleeding, in the midst of hard-hearted hirelings, the mark of scorn and violence, which move it not. Approach it not with flowers. Let the stern, sharp thorns remain. Strip them not off for such a substitute. The soldiers were mistaken when they thought to mock him. They have woven the noblest crown for the brows of suffering virtue. Let it stay — till it is changed by his own Father's hand for the crown of eternal joy and glory.

But there are crowns which monarchs, conquerors, and heroes wear: crowns of laurel for victors; crowns of gold and gems for reigning princes. Shall we not choose one of these, the greenest or the brightest, wherewith to crown our Lord? Who shall do it? Who will commit that essential error of the Jews, by treating the Messiah as a temporal conqueror or sovereign, or offering to him the emblems which are so coveted by them? Take away the toys. Let them not come into this hallowed presence. They would only show how dim and worthless they are, near to that unearthly majesty, and by the side of that crown of thorns. Take away the laurel wreath — it is stained with human blood. There is blood, too, upon the thorns — but it is the Saviour's own. It is his own blood which he now begins to shed for the liberty and the happiness of his brethren, and not the blood of his brethren, poured out after the manner of conquerors, for his own aggrandizement. It is his own blood, dropping down, not for dominion or fame, but for truth, and peace, and virtue. He fought; but not with carnal weapons, and not to enslave the bodies of men, but to emancipate their minds, and to redeem their souls.

He fought; not at the instigation of the lusts of the flesh, and in obedience to them, but undauntedly and perseveringly against them. He conquered; but not to increase the power of death, but to weaken and destroy it, to overthrow the hosts of darkness, to burst the bonds of sin and the grave. In this warfare he endured hardship, hunger, and thirst, pain, reproach, and contradiction. Humility, patience, meekness, long-suffering, forgiveness, — it was by these that the battle was fought and won. Take the laurel wreath away. It tells not of struggles and victories like these. The bare and rugged thorns are a more expressive and befitting crown for him who loved us and gave himself for us, and by his death destroyed death. Neither bring the gemmed diadems of royalty instead. They have been too much degraded and soiled by the hands which have usurped them, and the heads on which they have descended. They have clasped brains which were on fire with mad ambition, or teeming with dark schemes of tyranny. They have sat idly on heads which were empty of thought, or only thinking of some selfish indulgence; careless of others' wants, and studious only to create or gratify their own. Why should they be brought here? At best they signify but a partial, fluctuating, and temporary authority, however well improved and exercised, which human fancy and will may overturn, which a few hours may transfer, and which death will soon cover up in dust. Why then should they be brought here? Here is a king anointed directly from on high, with the unmeasured Spirit of God. Here is a ruler who rules over the spirits of men, and will rule forever; for his voice hath gone forth into all lands, his words unto the ends of the world. Here is a monarch unto whom power has been committed, real, permanent power, over nature, over fear, and over time. And it is through suffering that he holds it, and in endurance and self-denial that he exercises it: not consulting his own will, but that of his Father, nor his own ease, but the welfare of all men, yea, of his enemies. Here he stands, in the hall of a Roman viceroy, who, with all his power, has weakly, and against his own wish and judgment, surrendered a just and innocent one to a furious multitude and a bloody death. Here he stands, amid insulting cries and ferocious blows, supreme and kingly in suffering love; bound, and yet the only free one there; a prisoner, condemned to the cross, and yet redeeming countless spirits from captivity and death through the grace of his righteousness, and the royal might of his overcoming fortitude. Compare his crown of thorns with Pilate's royal cincture — and say which is the truest emblem of dominion, majesty, and victory. Is there not in every firm-set pointed thorn more self-conquest, more spiritual might, more endurance, and more victory, than ever glittered within the compass of a diadem? That twisted bramble is the true crown. Displace it not from the head of the conqueror of death, the redeemer of men, and the king of Israel.

Let that crown remain upon his head, as he passes out from before the dishonored chair of justice, reigning, though a prisoner and doomed to death, in calmness and dignity over the rude waves of the rushing crowd. Let it remain, as he proceeds through the streets, and on his way to Calvary, pale and weary, moving to tears and pitiful lamentations the daughters of Jerusalem, but quelling in perfect peace the crying emotions of his own nature. Let it remain, while he is nailed to the tree, and one after the other his hands and feet are pierced and lacerated; for his spirit holds dominion over the extremest pains which his flesh can be made to suffer. Let it remain, while they who pass by are wagging their heads and scoffing at him; he is far superior to such poor contumely. Let it remain, while that dying prayer is rising to heaven for the forgiveness of his enemies and deriders, for this is indeed an act of royalty, such as the world has never witnessed before. Let it remain, while the darkened sun and trembling earth are giving signs of their homage to the crucified Son of God. Remove it not from the cold brows, serene in death, till he is taken down from the cross and laid in the new tomb beneath. Then unbind it, that he may rest a Sabbath rest after his labor and his victory.

And let us learn from this crown of thorns, that there is majesty in sorrow, and that suffering is of itself a crown. Everywhere there is proof of this truth. Who has not been subdued and awed by another's mighty sorrow? Who has not been elevated by his own? It gives dignity and wisdom to the simple; brings reflection and sobriety to the thoughtless; and makes the humble and weak strong and invincible. The house of mourning is a palace, and they who enter its gates observe a reverential silence, or speak with reverence, as in the presence of majesty.

To resign ourselves in suffering to the will of our heavenly Father, is to sit down on the throne of his Son. It is especially so when we endure tribulation in the cause or for the sake of holiness. "Blessed are they who are persecuted for righteousness' sake, for theirs is the kingdom of heaven." To suffer for truth and virtue is to reign with celestial power, to govern with spiritual and divine prerogative. Desires and passions are ruled; fears are banished;

worldly interests surrender; vanities and pleasures fall down at our feet; truth flourishes, and virtue triumphs and looks up, when the soul has defied temptation and violence, and put on the crown of stern endurance. When we suffer with manliness and love, murmuring not, and reviling not, do we not wear our Saviour's crown, and share his kingdom, which is the kingdom of heaven?

And even when we suffer for our sins, if grief and pain bring consideration, which is their office, if sorrow work repentance, and if thus our excesses be cut off, our evil passions and habits be conquered, the rebellion of our perverted nature be subdued, and the recreant soul be led back submissive to God, then, too, will suffering be the sign of empire, and sit on our brows like a crown.

Thorns spring up in the various paths of all our lives. We cannot avoid them, nor prevent many of them from severely wounding us. But let us be comforted, yea, let us be thankful to know that we may weave them into crowns, "if we unite them to Christ's passion, and offer them to his honor, and bear them in his cause, and rejoice in them for his sake."

March 27, 1831.

SERMON XIX.

RECOGNITION OF FRIENDS.

Father, I will that they also whom thou hast given me be with me where I am.—*John* xvii. 24.

It is not from any vague or doubtful inferences that the Christian derives his belief of a future world. His faith is more direct and steadfast. Christ has risen from the dead, and become the first fruits of them that slept. The resurrection of our Lord, who was made in all things like unto his brethren, is an argument for man's immortality which, at the same time that it is more convincing than any which philosophy has urged, is so plain that its force is immediately acknowledged by the humblest understanding.

My object at present, however, is not to consider the proofs of a future existence, but, assuming the truth of the doctrine as revealed in the gospel, to ascertain how far it may encourage us in a belief of a reunion with our departed friends in heaven. It is an inquiry of the deepest interest. The hopes and fears which it involves are among the most powerful which can animate or distress the human bosom. The consolations which it may afford are among the highest and dearest which can be brought to affliction, when she sits in the dust and weeps for those who are not. Let us then inquire whether, after death, we shall, or shall not be forever united with each other.

Some, who perhaps have not duly considered this question, place it among those merely speculative ones, on which we can never hope in this world to obtain any satisfaction. Such are the questions: Where is heaven to be? What will be the occupations there? What kind of bodies shall we have, precisely? On these particulars we may form our several theories if we please, but there exist no real grounds for satisfactory conclusions. We must remain in ignorance; and it is of no great consequence that we should be informed. But the question, whether we shall rejoin and recognize hereafter those whom we knew and loved in this world, is of quite another character, of more interest and importance than those others, and admitting of a more easy and reasonable solution.

In support of this opinion, I will observe, in the first place, that the resurrection which is revealed in the gospel is a resurrection of individuals as individuals, of each person in his distinct personality. Few will maintain that comfortless system of antiquity, which teaches that the human soul is to be absorbed, after the death of the body, into the spirit of the universe. What satisfaction can it give us to know that we shall not be entirely lost in the great creation, if we are also to know that we must resign all separate perceptions and pleasures, and never must think, feel, or enjoy, as distinct existences?

It will be readily granted, therefore, that we shall live hereafter as separate and distinct individuals, — as truly so as we exist in the present life. And yet from this unpretending and almost self-evident postulate may clearly be deduced the doctrine, which some please to call a speculative one, of the reunion and recognition of friends in a future state.

If it be evident that we are to exist as distinct individuals, it is equally evident that we must know ourselves to be the same individuals who existed here. For, if we are not to be made certain of that, a resurrection will be equivalent to another creation, — to the formation of a race of beings with whom we, who now live on the earth, can have nothing to do. That the belief of a future state may exert the least influence over our conduct, it is necessary that we should also believe that we shall be able to identify ourselves then, with ourselves as we are now; otherwise our belief will furnish no motive to virtue, nor any consolation in adversity.

It is further evident, that, if we are to be conscious of our identity with our former selves, we must be conscious of the acts of our former existence; especially if we regard the future state as a state of retribution. For it is impossible to conceive how we can be the subjects of reward or punishment, without being sensible of what we had done or omitted on earth, to render us deserving of either. But, if we are to be conscious of the acts of our former existence, if we are to remember our conduct while we were on the earth, we must likewise remember those among whom we had our conversation, those who, in a great measure, made our conduct what it was. Our duties, virtues, faults, sins, and vices arise almost altogether from the relations of society. We cannot remember the one without calling to mind the other. They are inseparably united, and the imagination cannot disjoin them. If I should remember that I had done a particular injury on earth, I must remember him whom I injured. If I should remember that I had performed a particular act of benevolence, I must remember the person whom I assisted. How much more should I remember, in the review of my life, those with whom I had been connected in the daily and most intimate intercourse of life; those who had exercised the most efficacious influences in the formation of my character; those who had called forth and gained and kept the best affections of my heart. The recollection of my former self and my former associates must be produced together, and from the same principle. If the one be evident, the other is so too.

We have now a direct inference of the mutual recollection of friends in a future state, from the Christian doctrine of the resurrection of each individual to a distinct existence. And so well am I satisfied that the inference is rational and sound, that I could hardly tell which of the two doctrines I most firmly believed.

But the recollection of our friends, and a reunion with them, are not one and the same thing. There is still another step to be taken, from the one to the other. We may recollect our friends, and yet not be permitted to recognize or rejoin them. But is this probable? Can we for a moment suppose it? Will God disappoint our most cherished expectations? Will he condemn us to preserve in our memory the shadows of those we loved, while he denies to us their society and sympathy? Are we not only doomed to endure the pangs of separation from them here, but to know in the future world that when we left them here we lost them forever? The supposition is inconsistent with the goodness of our Creator, and should be dismissed as such. We shall not only remember, but rejoin, in the heavenly world, the friends from whom we had been transiently separated by death.

There is another course, yet more direct, if possible, than the above, which will bring us to the same conclusion. It involves no subtleties or minute discussions, and consists in the answer to as simple a question as could well be asked. The question is this: Are we, or are we not, in the world above, to live alone? Are we, or are we not, to lead, after death, an eternity of solitude? This is the only alternative. Each soul, in its glorified state, must either have a range entirely to itself, which shall never approach the sphere of any other soul, or it must associate with its kindred. It must exist in solitude or in society. Let any one put this plain question to himself, and he cannot hesitate in giving his answer. He will perceive that it is contrary to sound reason to imagine an eternal life of loneliness; and he will decide that the life of the blessed must be a life of society. And what society can it be but that of friends?

By whom shall we be surrounded but by our friends? With whom shall we live if not with our friends? What beings will be more likely to partake with us the joys of heaven than those who shared with us the joys and the sorrows of earth? What souls will be so probably associated with our own as those to which our own had been endeared and assimilated by education, habit, intercourse, and time? Among the innumerable hosts of heaven, shall we be denied the sight of those whom, of all others, we most wished to see? In the vast assembly of spirits, shall we search in vain for those whom we seek most eagerly? Will the only blank in creation be that which we are the most desirous to fill? Will the only wounds which are left unhealed be those which death had inflicted, and which we hoped that immortality would cure? Our feelings, our reason, our common sense, will at once reply that it cannot be so.

When we ask for scriptural evidence of the reunion of friends in a future state, are we not answered by every passage from Scripture which speaks of that state as a social one? And the fact is, that it is spoken of there in no other way. Whether the mention is incidental or direct, it constantly presents heaven to our thoughts as a place or state in which the righteous shall meet together, not exist separately. If we listen to Jesus, we hear him declare, that where he is his disciples shall be also. If we turn to the Epistles, Paul tells us that when Christ, our life, shall appear, we also shall appear with him in glory; and the writer of the Epistle to the Hebrews points with rapture to the "general assembly and church of the first-born, which are written in heaven." If we pass over to that grand vision which concludes the books of the New Testament, we hear in heaven "as it were the voice of a great multitude, and as the voice of many waters, and as the voice of mighty thunderings, and the voice of harpers harping with their harps." The blessed in heaven are always represented as being in society, as being with their brethren, with angels, with their Saviour, and with their God.

Now, hardly anything can seem to be plainer than that, as heaven is a social and not a solitary state, they who live together there must know each other, and that they who knew each other here must know each other there. And it is one of the most reasonable of all propositions, that, if we carry any affections with us into the future state, they will fly first of all to salute those who in this state were their cherished objects. When a mother joins the heavenly company of the redeemed, will she not, if she retain anything of her former self and nature, if she have not lost her identity and the consciousness of it, will she not ask for "the babe she lost in infancy?" If she be herself, she will ask for it. If God be good, she will find it, know it, embrace it. How she will find it, by what marks know it, and with what exercises renew her love, must be left for immortality to reveal; but the rest, the simple fact of recognition, is plain, — so plain that I am disposed to think that the reason why so little is said in the Scriptures of future recognition, is, that it was considered as naturally implied and involved in the fact of a future social state. On such a subject, intimation is equivalent to distinct declaration, and is sometimes even more forcible. Let us see if there be not such intimations of future recognition to be found in the Scriptures as amount to a declaration of the fact, because they cannot be fully explained except on a supposition of the fact.

Recognition is intimated by exhortations to comfort on the loss of friends. The burden of our sorrow in the loss of those whom we love, is, that we have lost their society, which was the very dearest thing on earth to us; the most applicable consolation which can be offered to alleviate this burden, is, that their society is not lost to us forever, that we shall enjoy it once more, that we shall meet again.

Now, what says St. Paul, in his Epistle to the Thessalonians? "I would not have you to be ignorant, brethren, concerning them which are asleep, that ye sorrow not even as others which have no hope. For if we believe that Jesus died and rose again, even so them also which sleep in Jesus will God bring with him." Beautiful words of assurance and comfort! How soothingly they fall on the wounds of the heart! Well counsels the apostle soon after, "Wherefore comfort one another with these words." And what makes them so peculiarly comforting? Not simply the assurance of restoration to life, a waking up of those who have fallen asleep, but the idea of collection, association, reunion, which the language supposes, and which is so pertinent to the case of separation to which they are addressed. As Jesus rose from the dead, even so God will awaken and bring *with* him those who slept in him; "and so," says the apostle, "shall we ever be with the Lord." We, who have been parted, shall again be united, and Christ shall be our head, and we shall part no more. That is consolation; consolation which exactly meets the case of distress.

To illustrate this by a comparison, let us suppose it to be necessary that a whole family, united by the tenderest mutual affection, should remove from the land where they had been brought up together to another land, which is distant indeed, but far better; and to be equally necessary that they should remove, not all together, but one by one, and that there should be an interval of a considerable space of time between each removal. When one member of this family departed for the place of his destination, what would be the most appropriate consolation which could be offered to those who remained behind? Would they be fully comforted by being told that he who had just gone away had gone to a country which enjoyed a more delightful climate than that which he had left, where he would live in health and at ease, and that they themselves would in due season be called to the same country, though to be sure they would live in different parts of it, and not be allowed to see each other any more? Would they be satisfied with this account of their dispersion, though it were to take place in "a land which is the joy of all lands"? It would be imperfect consolation compared with the assurance that, in that far, happy land, they were to be reunited, after the term of their temporary separation, and renew the intercourse which in a bleak clime and a barren country had constituted their joy and their wealth. That would be consolation; and such a reunion would be implied, and would naturally be considered as implied, if they were told by a sympathizing friend not to sorrow for their loss as the hopeless sorrow, but to look forward to the land where their relative had gone, and to which they were to be taken themselves.

Other passages besides the one above adduced might be quoted, containing intimations to the same purpose. They are not direct declarations of the fact of recognition; but we cannot read them without supposing that the fact was in the writer's mind, and that indeed he had no other thought on the subject but that he should certainly know, after the resurrection, those whom he had known before.

The scriptural evidence in favor of future reunion and recognition, with which the deductions of probability, the inferences of reason, and the dictates of the affections well coincide, amounts to this. Heaven is a social state. If we and our friends are found worthy of an entrance into that state, we shall form a part of its society, and consequently remember and know each other. They who were near to us here, if they are also near unto God, will be near to us there; and, other things being equal, they will be nearer to us than others, simply because we have known them more and longer, and loved them better, than others, and have associations with them so interwoven with our earthly or former life that they can scarcely be destroyed or disturbed except with our consciousness and memory.

Nor can I see that the restoration of friends to each other's society in a future state is inconsistent with that universal and heavenly love which will animate the bosoms of all the blessed. Particular affection for those with whom we have been particularly connected is not inconsistent with a kind and generous affection for many friends, for all the good from all ages and all countries of the world, to whom the better country will be the great and final meeting-place. The ground of this particular affection is, the relation which individuals have held toward each other in this life; and this life, though short in duration, and poor and unimportant when compared with the next, is yet the introduction to the next, the scene of probation for the next, the life in which our affections and virtues have been formed and educated, and have acquired their private associations; and it is therefore not to be supposed that all this is to be made a blank hereafter, as if it had never been. "And when we reflect," says Bishop Mant,[*]

---

[*] In a small volume entitled *The Happiness of the Blessed*.

"on the pleasure which is imparted to our minds by being admitted, after long separation, to the society of those whom we have known and loved from early years, but from whom we have been constrained to endure a temporary separation; and on the special delight which we experience from renewing, in communion with them, old but dormant affections, retracing in conversation the events of scenes gone by, and dwelling upon affairs of mutual personal interest, — a delight which the formation of no new acquaintance, however virtuous, however intelligent, however amiable, is for the most part found capable of conferring; it may be thought probable that, among their future associates, considered as constituents of the happiness of the blessed, those whom they have formerly known and loved and cherished will be comprehended, and that the company of the spirits of other just men made perfect will not preclude a readmission to the fellowship of their former connections and friends." In short, let it only be premised that friends are worthy of each other's love in heaven, and it is no more than rational to suppose that they will derive a peculiar satisfaction in each other's society there from the circumstances with which Providence had bound them together during their sojourn on earth.

But here an objection has been made, founded on the question of worthiness. If some with whom the good have been connected here below should, from their unworthiness, be excluded from the delights and the society of heaven, the good, it has been said, will, on the supposition of their knowing this, suffer pain; and pain cannot be suffered in heaven.

A few considerations may remove this objection. In the first place, though pain will not be suffered in heaven, there is no reason to believe that a certain degree of regret may not, and that this regret will be so consonant with our sense of justice that happiness will not thereby be essentially disturbed. Heaven is represented as a place where there will be "no more pain." This is in order to give an idea of its exemption from the accidents and deaths, the sorrows and alarms, to which we are subject here. But such a representation of future bliss by no means excludes the idea of imperfection. And if the soul is to make progress hereafter, and rise from glory to glory, and from one step of happiness to another, the idea of imperfection must be necessarily attached to such a state, because a state of improvement must needs be a state of imperfection. God himself is the only and absolutely perfect. If we are continually advancing nearer to him, we may be satisfied, grateful, and happy, whether on earth or in heaven; and infinitely more happy, doubtless, in heaven than on earth, on account of the many glorious circumstances which will attend our great change. But if we remember our former selves, we must remember our former sins of transgression and omission; and this remembrance will produce regret; and this regret, without preventing our enjoyment of heaven's felicities, will, together with other causes, maintain within us a constant humility, a virtue which will not lose its lustre and value amidst the brightest glories of the new Jerusalem. If, therefore, we may remember with regret our own past offences without losing the privilege of heavenly happiness, we may likewise view with regret the banishment of some of those with whom we were connected on earth by the ties of nature or habit, and yet be so enlightened with regard to the justice and beneficial ends of that banishment as not to experience therefrom any suffering which would embitter or be inconsistent with celestial blessedness.

Secondly, it must be considered that vile conduct does alienate brother from brother, and impair affection here on earth. May it not, therefore, be presumed that the good will not take with them into a future state any strong affection, or any other than compassion, for those whose vices have estranged affection, and weakened, if not broken, the bonds of nature and of love? "And it may be," again observes Bishop Mant, "since God's rational creatures are dear to him according to their moral excellence, and since the blessed in the future state will be 'like God'; it may be that their *affection* toward those who, in their earthly relation, were naturally the objects of it, will be regulated by this likeness to the Divine nature, and that, whilst it will be ratified, confirmed, and strengthened with respect to such as partake of their Father's blessing and are objects of his love, it will be annihilated with respect to those who are banished from his presence, and pronounced aliens from his affectionate regard." In one sense, God loves and must forever love all his creatures; but the love which he bears toward those who have remembered and kept his commandments must be of a different character from that which he bears toward those who have forgotten and disobeyed him. And so in a similar manner will the love which the beatified feel for those with whom they walk in heaven, as they have walked on earth, be different from the love which they feel for those who wandered from them on earth and meet them not in heaven. God's love for the latter demands their punishment, and the love of his servants toward them will not question its infliction. They will bow before the

Supreme Wisdom and Goodness. They cannot regard as their friends those who are not the friends of God. And in this view, it may be said that the righteous in the future world will have all their friends with them. They who are not with them cannot be their friends.

And yet memory will be faithful, and love may plead. And here I come to a consideration which may obviate the difficulty advanced better than any other, and on which, better than on any other, I like to dwell. Though I fully believe that the wicked will be punished hereafter, and will not undertake to deny that they may not retain their wicked dispositions, and thus bring on themselves perpetual punishment, I do not believe that their wickedness or their punishment is necessarily and inevitably eternal. I believe that God's punishments hereafter, as his chastisements here, are designed to be corrective; and that on many, if not on all, they will have a correcting, reforming, and consequently restoring influence. I also believe, according to apostolic teaching, that "charity never faileth"; no, not in heaven. And so I believe that it may extend its pitying and saving regards to those who most need them, to those who have made themselves outcasts from the heavenly country, the city of our God. In what errand, in what duty, can the blessed be more celestially employed than in bringing back, or endeavoring to bring back, into the family of the redeemed those erring and lost ones to whom nature had formerly bound and endeared them? May it not be one of the employments, one of the most glorious employments and crowning pleasures, of those who have been saved themselves, to be made instrumental in restoring others, who once were dear, to that peace of spirit which they have madly destroyed, to that heaven which they have justly forfeited? O who that has been found worthy to be a partaker " of the inheritance of the saints in light " would hesitate to forego for a time, and time after time, the society and the joys of his blissful abode, that he might work upon the heart of one whom he had numbered among his family on earth, and place him once more in the same mansion with himself? Who would not pray before the mercy-seat to be sent on such a mission of mercy? " Let me go," he might say, " let me go to the exile, and persuade him to return. He has suffered long. Long has he been wailing in outer darkness. Remorse must have visited his burning heart. Solitude and anguish must have broken down his perverseness. He was not always perverse and wicked. Through the long vista of ages I can see him as he once was. He once was a happy child, an innocent child, affectionate and ingenuous, and pure as the light which beamed from his eyes or played on his clustering hair. I have held him in my arms. I have watched his smiles and dried his tears. I loved him once. O that I might cherish him again! that I might bear to him thy forgiveness! that I might bring him back to happiness, to heaven, and to Thee!" Would not the Universal Father grant the prayer? Can it be proved to me that the saints and angels are not and will not be occupied in fulfilling his restoring purposes? Am I told that between the saved and the lost there is a great gulf fixed, so that they who would pass and repass cannot do so? I will not insist that this argument is drawn from merely the illustrative part of a parable which is not intended to convey either doctrine or fact, but will grant that there must needs be a profound separation between the happy and the wretched, the acquitted and the condemned, in a future state, — a separation which neither party can pass over at will. And yet, by the permission of the Almighty, and on messages of his own grace and compassion, that gulf may be passed; and what gulf can there be too wide for the wings of love, too deep or broad for the passage of charity?

The considerations which have been mentioned are abundantly sufficient, to my mind, to obviate the difficulty which they have been brought forward to answer. But if they were less convincing, if the difficulty remained in its full force, yet the doctrine of future recognition would not be disproved. No objection drawn from a probable state of painful feeling for the wicked could overthrow the fact that heaven is a social condition of being, on which fact the doctrine of the mutual recognition of friends in heaven still would rest unmoved. This fact should be sufficient to content and console us. Heaven is a social state, a city, a kingdom, a church, in which there is a great assembly, an innumerable company, and in which the innocent and good, the servants of the King Eternal, the spiritual and true worshippers of the Father, will meet together, and know each other, and never be separated any more. There the parent will see the child, improved by heavenly culture, and listen to the voice, now made more musical, which in days gone by was the sweetest music he ever heard. There the child will find the parent, and hear from him those words of love and wisdom which were early lost to him on earth. There brother and sister will meet again, and exchange again that confidence and sympathy which passed between them and united them here. There the widowed wife will meet the husband, and the husband the wife; and though they will be as the angels, where there is no marrying nor giving in marriage, the ties and affections of earth will not be forgotten, and in spirit they twain will be one.

Years soon finish their revolutions. A few more incidents, and the scene of mortal life is closed. Time hastens to restore that which we thought it was too hasty in demanding. Death promptly repairs as well as destroys, rejoins as well as divides, is cruel and kind in quick succession. "All the days of my appointed time will I wait," said the patient man, "till my change come." The last change cannot be long in coming to any. "All the days of my appointed time will I wait," is the language of every pious spirit, "till my change come." All the days are but few. I will wait and hope and cheerfully trust, till they are gone. The distance can be but small which keeps me from those whom I have loved and yet love, and, in the presence of God and my Redeemer, and in the light of heaven, shall continue to love forever.

> "Pass a few fleeting moments more,
> And death the blessing shall restore,
>   Which death hath snatched away;
> For me thou wilt the summons send,
> And give me back my parted friend,
>   In that eternal day."

NOTE.

The preceding discourse was never preached as one continuous sermon. It contains the substance of two sermons, one of which was written and preached as early as the year 1819, and the other in the year 1834, and both of which have been heretofore separately printed as essays, contributed by the author to different publications.

SERMON XX.

VOICES FROM HEAVEN.

And they heard a great voice from heaven saying unto them, Come up hither. — Rev. xi. 12.

AND we, too, hear voices from heaven, saying unto us, Come up hither. Did we not, how low and grovelling our desires, our pursuits, our very natures, would be! Did we not, what a dusty road our pilgrimage would run: hard to travel, and yet more hard to leave! How companionless our souls would feel on the way, as kindred souls departed, one by one! How silent and cheerless would be the night of our fortunes, and how transient and profitless their day! If the spirit were not spoken to from above, how it would cleave to things below; and how dependent it would be upon them, drooping when they drooped, and falling when they passed away; and how dark and destitute it would be in the hour of death! But now we do hear voices from heaven, saying unto us, Come up hither. And our wayfaring hearts are cheered, and the book of our life is interpreted, and our cares are rebuked and dispelled by those clear and noble voices. The spirit looks up as it hears their sound, the sound, as it were, of its native language; and feeling that it was not born from the earth nor for it, frees itself from earthly bonds, takes sweet counsel with household spirits, and rises to its native seats.

These voices, like that which the two unburied witnesses of the Apocalypse heard, are great voices, full of majesty and power, so that we cannot fail to hear them, if we have ears to hear.

There is, in the first place, a voice even from the lower and material heaven, calling on our souls, and urging them to ascend. The stars of the firmament, and the sun and the moon, speak as well as shine. They " utter forth a glorious voice "; a voice which not only declares the glory of God, but exhorts the spirit of man. The purposes of their creation, and their shining, and their singing, are doubtless manifold; but one purpose is to publish to mortals that there is something above and beyond the dark little globe on which they live and die; yea, that there are myriads of greater and brighter worlds. And what is this but to tell them not to be devoted, not to bind themselves down, not to pledge and wed themselves to that one spot, but rather to look higher and further, and see that there are other habitations, and other scenes, and other fields of action. With a great voice, the stars say unto our souls, Come up hither! Come up into the vast domains of space, and count our numbers, and compute our size, and bathe in our brightness, and learn what we can tell you of height and of depth, of splendor and of power. Stay not always below. Breathe not always in mists and vapors. Regard not earth so exclusively and so long as to rest in the conclusion that earth is all. But come up hither. Survey our host. Tarry a while in our company; and behold and see and remember that there is a universe above and around you. — Thus speak the stars. Their meaning is not to be mistaken. The simple fact, which our very eyes reveal to us, that over our world there are worlds innumerable, leads the spirit out from the narrow confines of the body and lifts it above the dust, which the body is and to which it must return, and gives it larger views, and inspires it with hopes which seek infinity and eternity. Listen to the holy stars. Listen in the still night. They watch while the world sleeps. By their light and their beauty and their vastness, by that elevation of theirs which is congenial to spirit, and addresses itself to spirit, they will speak to the soul that watches with them, and invite it upwards to themselves, where orb hangs above orb, and darkness is not, and the small and shaded earth may be for a time forgotten. Astrology is not altogether false. It was an old superstition, which has passed away, that the stars govern our mortal destiny. It is an eternal truth, which passes not away, that they assist in revealing to us our immortal destiny, by calling our souls up into the boundless region of the works of God.

2. We do not stop, however, but only begin with these works, all bright and eloquent as they are. They introduce us to him who made them; to him from whose fountain they draw their light, and of whose voice their own is but an echo. God delegates not to his creatures, but reserves as his own right, the highest converse with his likeness, the human soul. He is the Father of spirits, and he will speak himself to his children. And from the heaven where he dwelleth, he says to them, Come up hither. The hopes which he has imprinted within us so plainly and durably that doubt and fear cannot greatly obscure, nor vice itself completely erase them; the longings which we experience after a good, a glory, and a permanence which we find not here; the desire and

capacity of improvement which are never filled nor exhausted here; the affections which cannot rest here, but are attracted continually, though oftentimes insensibly upward; the thoughts which will be searching into the future, and turn not back at the gate of death, but keep on searching beyond the grave; the promises which are written in the pages of his recorded truth; the promises which are spoken by his repeated mercies and his communicated grace: all these are the sacred words of his lips, and the great voice from heaven with which he says to us, Come up hither. Come up into the spiritual dwelling-place of your Creator, and birthplace of your own souls. Consider not that state as your end which I have ordained to be your probation, nor that world as your home which I have made your pilgrimage. If you are tired in your journey, look forward to your rest. If the earth seems a wilderness, transport yourselves in spirit to the promised land. If the pleasures of earth are transitory, and the glories of earth are vain, contemplate the lasting and substantial delights of the "better country." Remain not so constantly in your temporal residence as to forget the way to that abode where my children are to live forever. Come up hither by faith now, that hereafter you may come in by sight. Come up by hope, that when hope shall disappear, it may be swallowed up in fruition. Come up by charity and good works done in the body, that when your bodies are resolved into dust, your souls may be prepared for that happy and holy kingdom into which sin and impurity cannot enter. Come up hither on the wings of prayer. Come up hither by the exercises of piety and the strength of divine love. Come, and see my face, and be to me as sons.

Let us listen to the voice of our heavenly Father, speaking to us from the heaven to which he bids us rise. Let us be grateful to him for the paternal solicitude which prompts him to call us. He would not invite us if he did not desire our presence. He would not seek our souls if he did not love them. He would not thus consult for our happiness if our happiness were not dear to him.

3. But there is another to whom we are dear, even his own Son, who dwells with his Father; and he also calls us from the same heaven, saying unto us, Come up hither! Here are the mansions which I have been preparing for my disciples. It was to secure to you this blessed rest, that on earth I endured poverty, reproach, and suffering; that I taught, toiled, and died; that I burst from the tomb and rose. For this great end did I come to you, that you might come up hither to me,

that, where I am, there ye might be also. Cause not my labor for you to be vain. I earned my reward, that ye might share it with me. I have entered into my inheritance, that ye might be fellow-heirs with me, and sit down with me, in my Father's kingdom. I would have more guests, more friends, more partakers of my glory. I would not lose one soul that I once bled to redeem. Come up hither. There is room for you, and for all.

Loud and audible is this voice of the Saviour. Its call to the spirits of men is constant, and never to be mistaken by those who will give it any heed. Why did he teach us of heaven, if it was not to be the portion of his disciples? Why did he teach us at all, if here is to be the end? He is the way; but whither, if not to heaven? He is the resurrection and the life; but why, if believers do not rise and live? He is the Captain of our salvation; but how, if his ransomed host pass not through the flood after their Leader? And how are we his followers, if we follow him not whither he has gone up on high? Come up hither, come up hither, is the great voice of our ascended and glorified Master to the multitudes who know, or may ever know his name. Let our ready and grateful answer be, Lord, we come. Saviour, we come. Whither thou hast gone, and where thou art, we know, and the way, too, we know. O that we may have strength and wisdom to persevere in thy footsteps, till we meet thee above with those who have already joined thee!

4. And now we hear other great voices from heaven, saying unto us, Come up hither! They are the voices of "the glorious company of the apostles," "the goodly fellowship of the prophets," "the noble army of martyrs," the innumerable multitude of saints and sealed servants of God, which no man can number, of all nations and kindreds and people and tongues. Come up hither! they cry, and witness our joys, and be encouraged by our success. Ages roll on, but our pleasures are ever new. Your years come to an end, but we have put on immortality. Your days and nights succeed each other, but there is no night here. Faint not at your tribulations; if we had fainted, we had not conquered. Behold our crowns and our palms. Fight the good fight, as we did; and then come up hither unto us, and swell our song of praise and victory, and join with us in ascribing blessing and honor and glory and power unto him who sitteth upon the throne, and unto the Lamb forever and ever!

Where the spirits of all the just and good and pious and constant of all past times are assembled, shall not the spirit of every Christian, of every rational man desire to be, and strive to go? Shall not theirs be the society of his choice? Shall not their abode be the country of his own adoption? Will he refuse a little labor for such a rest? Will he repine at a light sorrow, which may work out for him such a weight of glory? He will rather say,

> "This is the heaven I long to know;
> For this with patience I would wait,
> Till, weaned from earth and all below,
> I mount to my celestial seat,
> And wave my palm, and wear my crown,
> And, with the elders, cast them down."

5. There are few to whom I am speaking who do not hear other voices, yet which, though not more animating than the last, are, by the provision of God, nearer to the listening ear, and dearer to the soul. There are few who do not number in their families those whose places are vacant at the table and the hearth, but who are not reckoned as lost but only gone before. And when the business of daily life is for a while suspended, and its cares are put to rest, — nay, often in the midst of the world's unheeded tumult, — their voices float down clearly and distinctly from heaven, and say to their own, Come up hither! Our infirmities are relieved; our strength is renewed; our fears and doubts are flown away;

our sins are forgiven. We hunger and thirst no more. We are disquieted no more. Let not your spirits walk on in darkness; our darkness is all dispersed. Weep not for us; our tears are all wiped away. Forget not the duties which remain for you on earth; but neither forget us, who wait for you here. Hearken to us, and be comforted! Come to us when your journey is done!

The voices of the stars, and of their Maker, — of our Saviour, Christ, — of his glorified saints, — of our departed friends, — how great and inspiring they are! Can we follow harsh and vulgar voices when such as these are calling to us? Shall the lower world claim all our conversation when we may thus commune with the inhabitants, and with the God of heaven?

By all that is good, and pure, and holy, and rational, by the power of virtue and grace and love, and by a sound mind, let us be persuaded to listen most attentively, most earnestly, to those voices which best deserve the audience of the undying soul. They are always speaking; it is ours but to hear. Let our journeying spirits, as they travel onward through the various passages of mortal life, in its rough places or smooth, prize every sound which is borne to them from the mansions of their only rest.

JANUARY 1, 1832.

SERMON XXI.

THE GOOD REVEALED.

There be many who say, Who will show us any good? Lord, lift thou up the light of thy countenance upon us. — *Ps.* iv. 6.

"THERE be many who say, Who will show us any good?" The number of those who complain of their condition and of human life, as of a bare waste, destitute of solid good and happiness, was large in the days of the Psalmist, and is so still. The complaint is a serious one. On what is it grounded? Are there just causes for its so often repeated utterance? There must be causes, powerful and permanent causes, for a murmuring lament which has come down to us with the sounds of remote antiquity, and is heard even now amid the sounds with which the world is full. There must be causes for this; but are they justifying causes?

In order to ascertain this, we must observe who they are who bring the heavy charge against our life, — what manner of persons those are who say, Who will show us any good? Let us see what their principles are, and what is the main course of their conduct, and then we may be able to form a judgment of the causes of their complaint.

We shall be struck with the fact, in the commencement of our survey, that they who complain of the sad vacuity of life belong to very different and indeed opposite classes as respects principles and conduct. One class is that of the religious; the other, that of the indifferent and irreligious: the one full of religious conviction and sentiment, the other destitute of them. It is somewhat strange that two descriptions of persons, taking essentially different views of the ends of life, should thus unite in an accusation against it. It is especially strange that they of the first-named class, who believe that life is ordained and the world is governed by a beneficent Deity, should yet maintain that life and the world contain no good to manifest that beneficence. It is especially strange — is it not? — that they who do not need to have the existence of a merciful Father and a merciful Providence proved to them, who do not say, Who will show us a good, wise, and careful Creator? should yet say, Who will show us any good? And yet they do say so; and they not only say it, but they think it religious to say it; they deem themselves doing honor to their Maker when they say it.

In this last circumstance, however, we have a hint of the causes of their complaint. Why can they suppose it a part of religion to complain of this life? For no other reason, surely, than because they express thereby a faith in something higher, better, more satisfying. Their complaint, then, is only an exaggeration of religious sentiment; the truth of the frailty of everything human, and the transitoriness of everything earthly, carried into excess, and turned into error — error, which, but for its origin, would be sin. Can we not say that imperfection intrudes into all that is human, and death often interrupts and soon will terminate all the enjoyment of earth, and the soul cannot be fully satisfied with what is temporal, — can we not say this without saying, Who will show us any good? Can we not say, that all which is merely worldly is vain; that the life which is devoted to the world is a life lost; that a soul immersed in worldly pursuit and pleasure is a soul drowned; that sin has filled the world with sorrow, and that there is no safe rest and no unbroken peace but in heaven, — can we not utter these truths, these solemn and momentous truths, without spoiling their truth and their religion by saying, Who will show us any good? This want of discrimination between what is frail and what is worthless; between what is of the earth, earthy, and what is on the earth but comes from heaven; between the good which is perverted and the perversion of that good, — is the cause why religious persons are found among those who disparage the whole scene of mortal life in all its aspects. They do not, in principle, disagree with those who look on life more cheerfully, and speak of it more thankfully; and therefore they should be exhorted, in the spirit of brotherly love, to consider that it is far from necessary to deny all good to the present life, in order to express their conviction that there is another which is better; or to maintain all created things to be evil, in order to enforce the truth that the Creator is the only good. They should be exhorted, moreover, to ponder the question, whether they are not injuring religion by appearing to join with the irreligious in their estimate of the human condition; and by inducing some to think that there is a natural affinity and union between religious views and gloomy views; and by leading others to ask in fearful doubt or despondency, whether God did really intend to place man in a world from which all good was excluded. Let them hold earth as cheap as they please, in comparison with heaven, — every pious spirit will sympathize with them in this, — but do not let them speak as if earth were unvisited by the goodness of God, — as if the footstool caught no rays from the throne.

But though the religious, from an error in the application of religion, sometimes speak too disparagingly and mournfully of human life, they are not apt to speak so bitterly of it as do the indifferent and irreligious. Oh, that bitterness, that scoffing, blistering bitterness! how much worse is it than only moanings and tears, however mistaken those moanings and tears may be. I do not know a state of mind from which we should more anxiously pray to be forever saved, than that which, scorning all that awakens other minds to gratitude or enkindles them into adoration, deliberately asks, Who will show us any good? It either evinces a coldness and hardness which no favors can affect, or a satiety which has lost all relish for calm and virtuous pleasures. What can induce such a state of mind?

Can it be that life has really been to these complainers a lot of unmitigated ill? Has a more than usual share of inevitable misery been the portion of their cup? It does not seem to be so. They have not suffered more than others have who do not complain at all, and who acknowledge and are thankful for a great amount of good. Have they been so situated that they have witnessed no good in others, no kindness, no self-denial, no self-sacrifice? This can hardly be. They have been in precisely the same situations in which others have stood who have beheld unnumbered instances of this description of good, and with a swell of the heart and a starting tear have blessed them. What is the reason, then, that these complainers can see no good in life, and request that it may be shown to them, as something which has not yet been discovered? Is it an irreligious forgetfulness of all benefits received, and of all graces and virtues witnessed? Tell me, complainer, hast thou never seen a bright day, nor felt a light heart? Hast thou never tasted food that was pleasant, or sleep that was refreshing? Hast thou never been the object of a father's care, or a mother's love, or a labor of kindness, or a word of encouragement? Has no one ever watched over thee, or worked for thee, or prayed for thee, or defended thee? Hast thou never seen one tear of pity or of thankfulness? Hast thou never seen a parent suffer that a child might be saved from suffering, or a man rescuing his fellow-man from want or from sin? I will not believe that thou hast not experienced and seen these things. Thou hast experienced, thou hast seen, and thou hast forgotten them, ungratefully forgotten them. Where is thy memory? where is thy justice? where is thy heart?

And sometimes is not this discontent the fruit of an inordinate self-esteem? Is it not sometimes the case that a man will allow nothing to be good because he thinks that nothing is good enough for such an one as himself? Are there not those who are constantly vexed by the thought that they always deserve more than they ever obtain, and that all benefits and blessings are but half-payments for their own merits? How much good would be revealed, how much happiness would be secured to them, by the aid of a little humility — that enlightening, soothing virtue of humility.

But the largest and sorest class of irreligious complainers are those who, by a course of unrighteous excess, have brought themselves into that most desolate region of satiety, where everything is faded and tasteless, nothing is beautiful, nothing is good. They have tried life, they say, and have found it disappointing and valueless; they have tried men, and have found them deceitful and selfish. Tried life! tried mankind! And how have they tried them? They have abused good, and changed its nature, and turned it into evil, and then complained that the evil was not good. They have sought for happiness where experience and conscience and God forbade them to seek for it, and then complained that there was no happiness. They have broken the laws of enjoyment, and then complained of the consequences of broken laws. They have dulled and deadened their physical and moral sensibility to rational and pure enjoyment, and then complained that there was nothing to enjoy. By acting continually on the selfish plan themselves, they have, as it were, compelled men to be selfish in self-defence, and then complained of their own work. They have frightened purity away from them by their impurity, and holiness by their taunts, and tenderness and devotion by their coldness, and then complained that they were lonely. They pervert, they reject, they banish the best blessings of life, and then they ask, Who will show us any good?

I have intimated what are some of the chief causes of the charge which is not uncommonly preferred against our human condition. It may be added that the complaint is sometimes of a temporary character only, — the sudden cry of a struck and wounded heart, — the voice of grief as it sits in darkness, and is unable for a time to discover any good through the veil by which it is shrouded. Of this we need only say, that it is the mistake of burdened and bewildered feeling, which will presently be rectified by that feeling itself.

But what answer shall be given to the complaining question, from whatever quarter or cause it may proceed? It is observable that the Psalmist gives no direct answer to the many who say, Who will show us any good? His implied answer is a prayer; "Lord, lift thou up the light of thy countenance upon us." But the answer implied in this invocation is full and complete. Only let the light of the Lord's countenance be lifted up upon us, only let us see God in all things, and all things in God, and then we shall never be tempted to say, Who will show us any good? Life will be full of good; blessings will glitter out from the recesses and by-paths of our condition, which before lay hidden in shadow; and our contentment, submission, and cheerfulness will be the practical answer to those who may persist in saying, Who will show us any good? The prayer is not, Lord, show us, or give us good, but, lift thou up the light of thy countenance upon us. The good already given, already existing, will then show itself, will glow all around us under that copious and hallowed light, and our countenances will reflect the beams which shine from the countenance of God.

Come, ye doubtful and ye disconsolate, whoever ye are, come and look upon the scene of life as it lies spread out in the light of a present Deity. God is there, and in his light you will see light. Look upon the human condition as a condition which he has ordained; look upon human trials as trials which he has appointed; look on human affections as implanted by him and struggling after him; on human sorrows as sent by him that they may lead weak and wandering souls forward and up to him; and on this world of human creatures, with all their joys and griefs, pursuits and interests, as passing away indeed, but passing away under his eye, that it may pass into a state more exalted and enduring;—look thus, I say, upon life and the world, and you will not ask, Who will show us any good? but you will exclaim, It is all good!

I will not ask you to fix your attention upon that which bears the common name of good. I will not ask you to look upon the fresh delight of childhood; on the open face of honesty; on the unwearied exertions and sacrifices of love; on the right hand of dispensing benevolence, the deeds of which its left hand is not permitted to know; on the patriot's devotedness, on the martyr's constancy: but I will ask you to contemplate things which are not so commonly called good. Look with me on the low places of poverty,—if those low places have the light of God's countenance upon them,—and you will see industry bringing health and contentment, and self-denial educating the soul, and privations borne with a patience which assures the mind at once of its own strength, and of a strength greater than its own. You will see more thankfulness expressed for a little than you will often see elsewhere rendered for an over-abundance, and more aid imparted from that little than you will often see elsewhere doled out from hoards. And you will call this good. Look again with me into the chamber of sickness. Pain is there, but in the divine light you behold it engaged in a holy and blessed ministry, subduing and softening the spirit, and clearing away the films from the spirit's eyes. The body is emaciated, but the soul is enlarged. The corporeal powers and functions are disorganized, but the mental powers are in orderly and harmonious action, or resting quietly upon God. And friendship and love are there, with more touching loveliness than they ever wore in gayer scenes; watching night after night, and yet feeling no want of sleep; pouring out attentions like unvalued water, which yet could not be bought with gold; hanging as if with their own existence on every variation of symptom and pulse in the beloved, and yet resigning the event to supreme wisdom. These things are there, and you must say that they are good.

Come, then, now, for now you are prepared, into the abode of death. Why is it not dark with unbroken darkness? Because the light of God's countenance is there, dispersing the darkness. Death is there; but in the light of the living God, what is death? The end of toil, the completion of the appointed task, the winning of the race, the rest after the battle, the passage into eternal life. Death is there, but so is the victory in which it is swallowed up. There is rest on that pale countenance; and a smile is there which the victorious spirit left upon the lips as it ascended to its Father and its God. You may say what you will of the joys of life; you may set upon them an estimate too low or too high; but if you have any feeling of those direct revelations of peace and triumph and eternal repose which are unfolded by the departure of the righteous, you will acknowledge that the greatest good has been shown to you in the chamber of death.

Poverty — sickness — death: these are generally enumerated as among the chiefest of evils. I have not undertaken to say that they are not evils, or that under certain circumstances they may not be dreadful evils; but in answer to the question, Who will show us any good? I have undertaken to demonstrate that good was to be found in all their several abodes. If in connection with poverty, sickness, and death there is a spirit of holiness, a pious and Christian spirit, which is the lifting up of the countenance of God, then is there a true and sublime good proceeding from them, which cannot elsewhere be surpassed. And if good, abundance of good, is to be discovered in these unpromising quarters, why not in other portions of man's condition and experience?

Doubtless there are evils; but many things are called evils, and dreaded as such, which a human spirit ought to be ashamed so to call and dread; and many things which are really evils are invested with their evil character by ourselves. Intemperance; licentiousness; man's stony want of feeling for his brother-man; ingratitude; the disappointment and misery which a child may cause to a parent, a husband to a wife, a wife to a husband: these are evils which cannot be diminished, and need not be magnified by any art of words. There is no good in them. But why? Because where they are the light of God's countenance is banished by transgression, and the darkness in which they lie may be felt. I cannot engage to find good in these. Nor will I engage to find good where multitudes rush for it, — in the abodes of revelry, in the haunts of excess and guilty pleasure. I do not expect to find good in any place where the light of God's countenance is not, and where God's word declares, as well as man's experience, that good cannot be. But wherever that light can shine, within the round of human suffering as well as of human enjoyment, there is good. And if we would find good, if we are honestly and earnestly seeking it, there is one simple rule to guide us to the object of our searchings. We must look for the pure shinings of that light; and instead of idly and querulously asking, Who will show us any good? we must humbly ask that the light may be lifted up upon us, and then all will be enlightened, and all will be good.

June 21, 1835.

SERMON XXII.

WALKING BY FAITH.

For we walk by faith, not by sight. — *2 Cor.* v. 7.

In certain respects, all men, whose mental faculties are in a sane condition, walk by faith; and in certain respects, all men, whose bodily eyes are open and uninjured, walk by sight. No man is such a universal sceptic, such a sense-bound infidel, that he does not believe many things which he does not and cannot see; nor is any man so complete a theorist, so wild a spiritualist, that he does not regulate his movements, for the most part, by the evidence of his eyesight.

Many a person thinks he believes nothing, has no faith, when in fact he believes a great deal, though not so much as he ought. He believes that there is a thinking principle within him; yet this thinking principle he never saw, nor touched, tasted, heard. He believes in the existence of past ages, and of multitudes of beings who lived in them; but these he never saw. He believes that millions of men now occupy the earth, whom he cannot see. He believes that other millions will occupy it when he is dead, and can see no more. So far from not possessing the eyes of faith, or making no use of them, he looks round the great globe with them, and searches into the mighty past, and gazes upon the unknown future.

The geologist walks by faith. It is faith and not sight on which he rears his knowledge and fame. He finds, imbedded in rock, certain portions of rocky substance, in the form of large bones. Rocks in the shape of bones: this is all that they are to his bodily eyes; and what they are to his eyes, they are to the eyes of the simplest and most unlettered beholder. Here is the whole story, from beginning to end, which they tell to sight. But faith guides the geologist back to the time when these stones in bony form were bones indeed, and clothed with sinews, flesh, and skin; and, as they are too large to have belonged to any animals such as we see, faith gives them to animals such as we do not see, and exhibits to his wondering mind gigantic creatures wandering and wading through the tall reeds of a miry and dimly lighted world, long ages on ages before that modern being, man, had, or could have had, his dwelling in it. Their very shapes are pictured to his imagination; and he can say what animals now existing they most resemble; and he can follow them through their trampled pastures till a great ruin overwhelms them, and their organized remains are consolidated among the rocks of a world which is in earnest preparation for his own upward-eyed race, — a race which will walk by faith, and not, as those dull and monstrous brutes have walked, by sight.

The astronomer walks by faith. The stars which present themselves to his sight are glittering points; and so they are to the eyes of all. And even when he uses his telescope, though they are multiplied, they are not magnified, but still remain glittering points. Faith, with feet which disregard the distance, and with eyes which can endure the splendor, leads him out among them, and he beholds them, no longer points, but a perpetually increasing multitude of magnificent suns, giving light to a yet greater multitude of revolving worlds. As such he speaks of them, confidently, as if he had so seen them; and yet, with the eyes of his body, he sees no more of them than the peasant sees, or the child.

The mariner walks by faith. He commits himself and his vessel and his property to the heaving surface of an ocean which is without a track, and trusting to the faithfulness of a balanced needle, seeks a country which he has never seen, to deal with people of whose existence his eyes have never certified him. All that weary way, through clear and stormy weather, by night and by day, over the unsounded and mysterious deep, among all its wonders and dangers, by faith in his needle, by faith in sun, moon, and stars, by faith in the invisible winds, by faith in what men have told him, he pursues his voyage, and arrives at the unknown shore.

If these and many others, indeed all others, walk, in certain respects, by faith, why should not Saint Paul and his fellow-believers, in his own and in all times, walk in other respects by faith? What is there unreasonable, out of the common course, contrary to analogy, in a Christian's walking by faith? In the ordinary concerns of life, in his every-day transactions, in going from house to house, in all those cases in which his eyes were given him for guidance, he walks, as others do, by sight. Why, then, should it be accounted strange, that, in paths where eyes are of no use, paths which transcend visible limits, and stretch off beyond familiar scenes and the world of sense, he should walk by faith? Are not others constantly doing the same, — walking, though not perhaps in his track, yet in tracks of their own, by faith, and not by sight? May he not walk by faith, as well as the geologist, the astronomer, the mariner?

Ah! but it will be said, the faith of the geologist, the astronomer, the mariner, s faith founded on evidence, on deduction, on testimony. Well; and is not the faith of the Christian founded on evidence, on deduction, on testimony? I know not of any weaker grounds on which true faith is founded. And the evidence is of the strongest, the deduction is of the clearest, the testimony is unexceptionable. Does the geologist, from the examination of organic remains, deduce the fact of an ancient form of the world, furnished with its peculiar inhabitants? If he be a Christian also, he deduces, from every organization which he beholds, the far more important fact of the existence of a wise and supreme Mind, which, before and above all other beings, prescribed their substance and structure, and pronounced the laws of their life. Does the astronomer, from the analogies of our own solar system, infer that twinkling stars are glowing suns, and that the intervening space is divided by the circles of dependent globes which rush and roll around their central luminaries? If he be a Christian also, he pursues a far higher inference, and finds Eternal Love presiding over its own creations, and an Eternal Providence, which acknowledges no remoteness, watching everywhere; and therefore, as he follows faith from world to world, he not only wonders, but adores. Does the mariner trust to the evidence of voices or books, when he launches forth to seek men and countries which he has never seen? If he be a Christian also, he trusts; and why should he not trust to the evidence of faithful men for information which much more deeply concerns him, — for information concerning One who came into the world that the world might be redeemed from sin, and that sinners might be restored to holiness; of One who died that our evil passions might be nailed to his cross; of One who rose from the dead, and entered into glory, that we might rise from sloth and worldliness and spiritual death, and seek a country above, where the leaves do not wither, and the fruits do not fall; where joys are pure and lasting, and sin and death cannot come? On this information the Christian relies, to this evidence he yields his trust; and, spreading his sails and seizing his helm, he seeks, over the troublous waves, and through the changing skies of life and time, that blessed land of truth and peace which lies beyond them.

And why should he not? Why should he

not ground his faith on the evidence of those men? Did ever men speak more honestly? Has their veracity and trustworthiness ever been disproved? Were not their lives without reproach, and conformed to the facts of which they were the witnesses; and were not their souls filled with love and benevolence such as could have been fashioned after but *one* model; and were they not consistent and steadfast in their testimony, and did they not seal it with their blood, looking to a reunion with their risen Lord in the heavens? What is the matter with their evidence, that it should not be relied on? Search the world over, and no better evidence will be found. And when the ends of this evidence are considered, the great ends of redemption and immortal life, the collected records of human history contain not any evidence on any subject which can for a moment be compared with it.

Yet other evidence the Christian has on which to found his faith, which the others have not, and cannot have, for their extinct races, for their suns and worlds, for their distant voyages. He has the evidence of his heart, of his best and highest affections. The geologist may ask of his heart some knowledge concerning that strange and ancient earth into which he is prying, and it will answer him not a word. The astronomer may ask his heart concerning that marshalled host of shining spheres, and his heart will not add a feather's weight of testimony to that which he has already received. The mariner may inquire of his heart for tidings of the land to which he is going, and his heart will keep silence, for it can tell him nothing. But let the heart be questioned in simple earnestness concerning the Son of Man as he is described by the evangelists, and it will answer promptly that the description is true, and the person real; for no art or fancy could have pictured a character like his. Let the heart be asked whether he who was crucified rose again, and is the resurrection and the life, and it will reply that it sees his glory, and waits his judgment; that such a being could not have been detained in the cold arms of death, but has surely risen from the grave, and is set down on his throne. Let the heart be asked whether earth is enough, whether its joys are permanent, its pleasures satisfying, its peace unbroken; and it will return a mournful negative to the appeal. And let it be asked whether there is a heaven for virtue and holiness; whether there is forgiveness for contrition and repentance; whether all that was excellent and elevating in the souls of those whom we loved perishes with the body, or lives with God; and the questioned heart will answer from its fulness, that earth will claim its own, and heaven its own; that dust will return to dust, and the spirit to God; that they who have loved their Saviour have followed their Saviour, where they will enjoy his presence for evermore. The heart never resigns the objects of its pure regards; it cannot give them up; the grave claims them in vain. The heart sees them; the heart hears them; the heart clings to them always. And the unperverted heart, the honest, affectionate heart, adds its full testimony to the voice of revelation, and bears witness that God lives, and Christ is risen, and the souls of men cannot die; that things seen are temporal, and things unseen eternal; that realities are on the other side of the grave, and not on this; that shadows are here, and that truth and light are there.

"We walk by faith," says the apostle, "and not by sight." We are guided by the things eternal, rather than by the things temporal. We pursue the realities, rather than the shadows. We fasten our hold on that which is permanent, rather than on that which our sight itself may tell us is passing away. In the concerns of our souls we regard the author of our souls, and not the enemies of our souls. We strive to conform our conduct to the commandments of God, rather than the custom of the time. We keep our hearts fixed on the world which is to come, and the glories which will be revealed, rather than on the present world, which soon will be no more, and its objects, which will soon vanish from our eyes. This is the declaration of Saint Paul; and the way which he adopts and announces is the only true, and rational, and living way. The Christian has far more reason, more evidence and better authority for walking by faith, in the path of conduct and the regulation of life, than they who question or wonder at him can have for walking by sight. In his turn he may question and wonder at them. Why, he may ask, do you walk by sight? Why, formed to look upward, are you continually bending your spirit towards earth? Why do you confine your hope, that divine and soaring faculty, to fleeting objects, which perish while you pursue them? Why do you bind your affections so tightly to things which, though visible, are visibly withering, and which, even if they should remain, cannot follow you, cannot be taken with you, out of the world? Why do you look for your friends among the dead, — as if the clods of the valley could bury goodness, or hide and cover sin? Are you yourselves going nowhere but to the grave, which necessarily bounds and terminates every earthly prospect? Alas! that all your sight, that all your evidence, should be shut up there, should end by conducting you there! Is there no

God, no Christ, no resurrection, no immortality? Is the short life of sense more worthy than the eternal life of the soul? Oh, why do you walk by sight?

My friends; do we walk by faith? Do we walk as if there were other things in existence beside what we see, and of far more glory and desirableness than what we see with our mortal sight? Do we walk as if Christ had risen from the dead, and revealed another world to our souls, in comparison with which this world is nothing, but in preparation for which this world is everything? Let us ponder with ourselves that question. And let us remember that the question is not, whether we merely believe in God, in Christ, in the unseen and spiritual world, but whether we mould our dispositions, our purposes, our actions, after the image of that belief; not merely whether we *have* faith, but, more especially, whether we *walk* by faith; whether, believing in God, we walk in the way of his commandments; whether, believing in Christ, we walk as he walked, in benevolence, self-denial, and piety; whether, believing in his resurrection, we acknowledge its power, and rise from our sins, and set our affections on things above.

APRIL 15, 1838.

SERMON XXIII.

LESSONS OF AUTUMN.

The grass withereth, the flower fadeth; but the word of our God shall stand forever. — *Isaiah* xl. 8.

THE prophet of the old dispensation is quoted by an apostle of the new. "The grass withereth," — thus the solemn strain is echoed by the apostle Peter, — "and the flower thereof falleth away; but the word of the Lord endureth forever."

It appears to me that these sublime words, so full of pathos and of trust, must have been written by the one, and repeated by the other, in that season of natural decay when the grass was withering, and the flower was fading in their sight, when they saw with human sensations that all the greenness and beauty of earth was passing away, but felt at the same time, as servants of the Most High, that the truth and promises of their God were above change, and would endure forever.

Year after year, from the time of the apostle, from the time of the prophet, from an earlier time than his, the same untiring chant has been uttered by the withering grass and the fading flowers. The feelings excited by the autumnal season are unvaried, but they are so true, so deep, so near to the fountains of our life, that they are always fresh, always powerful. Time after time we may go into the autumnal woods, and, while the yellow leaves fall slowly down and touch the earth with a sound so soft that it is almost silence, the self-same thoughts shall be suggested to us, and yet without appearing hackneyed or old. They shall be as affecting the last time as the first. They shall even, like the words of fine poetry, or of ancient prayer, endear themselves by repetition. Are they not poetry? are they not prayer? When nature and the heart converse together, they converse, like old friends, on familiar and domestic things, on truths which cannot lose their interest, — the common but eternal truths of mortality. So complete is the system which runs through the visible universe, that there are evident analogies and sympathies between our mortal condition and the condition of all outward things. These analogies and sympathies are the same in every age. They are observed, felt, uttered, in every age. The utterance of them is transmitted from mouth to mouth. They often arise to the same heart and the same lips; but man cannot weary of the final truths of his mortal condition. They are his poetry — his prayer: his poetry, while they rest in the present world; and his prayer, when they are united with the future, and with God.

And what are the suggestions of autumn? What do we think, and what do we say, when we behold the leaves falling, the grass withering, and the flower fading? The peasant, as he pauses in his toil; the cottage-dame, as she sits at her door; the man of business, when he quits the paved and crowded streets; the young as well as the old; ay, and the giddy and gay as well as the serious: all express essentially the same sentiment which poets express, and which the prophet proclaimed, and the apostle repeated, long centuries ago. "All flesh is grass," says the prophet, "and all the goodness thereof is as the flower of the field." "For all flesh is as grass," repeats the apostle, "and all the glory of man as the flower of grass." That is the moral which never tires. That is the feeling which is as old as the time when the first leaf fell dry and shrivelled at the feet of the first man, and as recent as the present season of decadence and death. The conviction that all the goodliness of man's mortal frame, that all the glory of man's earthly prospects, hopes, and plans, is the beauty of withering grass, and the array of perishing flowers, is borne to all hearts by the sighing winds of autumn. Oh bond unbroken between nature's frailest children and ourselves! who is not conscious of its reality and its force? Oh primitive brotherhood between herbs and blossoms, and the sons of men; between the green things which spring up and then wither, and the bright things which unfold and then fade; between these, and countenances which bloom and then change, eyes which sparkle and then are quenched, breathing and blessed forms which appear in loveliness and then are gone! who does not acknowledge its claims of kindred? "Surely the people is grass;"—surely, there is no more stability in the strongest of mankind than in "the grass of the field, which to-day is, and to-morrow is cast into the oven."

Go into the fields and woods, when "the wind of the Lord" has blown upon them; when the blasts and the frosts of autumn have been dealing with them. A change has passed over everything, from the loftiest and broadest tree of the forest down to the little wild plants at its roots. Winged seeds are borne about by the fitful gusts. Leaves descend in dark showers. Dry and bare stems and stalks hoarsely rattle against each other, the skeletons of what they were. You cannot raise your eyes, but you look upon the dying; you cannot move, but you step upon the dead. Leaves and flowers are returning to the dust; can you forbear thinking, that, in this universal destiny, they are like yourself? Dust *thou* art, and unto dust thou shalt return. Can you forbear thinking that the successive generations of men, like the successive generations of leaves and flowers, have been cut off by the death-frost, and mingled with common earth? And are not individual names whispered to your memory by the dying fragrance and the rustling sounds, — names of those who flourished, faded, and fell in your sight? Perhaps you think of the fair infant, who, like the last tender leaf put forth by a plant, was not spared for its tenderness, but compelled to drop like the rest. Perhaps your thoughts dwell on the young man, who, full of vigor and hope, verdant in fresh affections, generous purposes, and high promise, and bearing to you some name which means more to the heart than to the ear, — friend, brother, son, husband, — was chilled in a night, and fell from the tree of life. Or perhaps there rises up before you the form of the maiden, delicate as the flower, and as fragile also, who was breathed upon by that mysterious wind, lost the hues of health, and, though nursed and watched with unremitting care, could not be preserved, but faded away. You are not alone in the brown woods, though no living being is near you. Thin and dim shades come round you, stand with you among the withered grass, walk with you in the leaf-strewn path. Forms of the loved, shades of the lost, mind-created images of those who have taken their place with the leaves and flowers of the past summer, — they speak not, they make no sound; but how surely do they bear witness to the words of the apostle and the prophet, till you hear their burden in every breeze, — the spontaneous dirge of nature. "The grass withereth, the flower fadeth," is the annually repeated strain from the fields and woods; and man's heart replies, "All flesh is grass, and all the goodliness thereof is as the flower of the field." The listening Psalmist heard the same theme and the same response, and he, too, has repeated and recorded them. "As for man, his days are as grass; as a flower of the field, so he flourisheth; for the wind passeth over it, and it is gone, and the place thereof shall know it no more."

But does the psalmist or the prophet or the apostle stop at these melancholy words, and close his lips after the utterance of such plaintive tones? Neither of them does so. How could inspired and faithful men, servants of

God, proclaimers of truth and religion, stop at the boundary of decay? They pass immediately from the truth of death to the truth of life. "But the word of our God," says the prophet, "shall stand forever." "But the word of the Lord," says the apostle, "endureth forever." "But the mercy of the Lord," sings the royal bard, "is from everlasting to everlasting upon them that fear him." Happy will it be for us, if, while we feelingly perceive the transitoriness of nature and of man's mortal state, we acknowledge the steadfastness of God's word, and the everlasting mercy of his providence. That which passes away should speak to us of that which remains. The constant rotation of decay is an intimation of the Being who ever lives to superintend it; whose throne decay cannot harm, because decay itself is his ministering servant. The certainty of death reveals an eternal word which commands death, and which both killeth and maketh alive. Let that word be our trust, even when we look on the withering grass, and think of the perishing children of men. Let it be our trust, as it was the trust of those "holy men of God, who spake as they were moved by the Holy Ghost"; and as it always is the trust of those who behold the operations of that same Spirit in all the signs of the universe, and feel its promptings in all the nobler aspirations within them. If we cannot trust in verdure, freshness, beauty, which soon languish and fail, in goodliness and glory, which fade and pass away, let us trust in the word which ordains their vanishing and departure; for that word is above them, and must endure. If the soul has any trust, — and oh, how it wrongs its nature and neglects its endowments when it has no trust, — it must place that trust in something which abides. What is abiding, but the word of God? "The grass withereth, the flower fadeth; but the word of our God shall stand forever."

The very grass itself as it withers, and the flower as it fades, seem to express such a trust, in their humble manner, and to inculcate it on their withering and fading human brethren. How quietly the grass withers! How submissively the flower bows its head on its stalk; how sweetly it exhales its last odors; how peacefully it fades! Nature dies gently. Listen! Do you hear any discordances in her parting sighs? They are all harmonious, — as musical, though with a different character, as the melodies of spring. You may be affected with sadness as you listen, but it is a sadness which soothes and softens, not disturbs and terrifies. I can sympathize with the man who relieves his full heart by weeping amidst the autumnal emblems of human dissolution; but I must only wonder at him if he weeps tears of anguish or despair. I could not weep so, surrounded by such mild and uncomplaining monitors. I perceive that the honors of the forest are resigned without a struggle. Wherever I turn, all is acquiescence. There is no questioning the will of Heaven. There are no cries when the leaves part from their stems, and sink to the ground. How can I do violence to the spirit of submission and trust which is diffused about me? It rebukes my misgivings, if I have indulged any; it silences my repinings, if unthinkingly I have uttered any; it steals into and hushes my heart. Why should we not receive the lessons which nature is, even though unconsciously, teaching us? Why should we break the general peace? Let us trust in the word of God, though it sends forth the decree, "Return, ye children of men!" Frail, fading, perishing, — what are we without trust? The support of the soul is trust in God, trust in the eternal, undecaying word of God.

And in nature's decline at this season, it may be observed further, there is not only the expression of quiet submission, but of hope and joy, — such joy as they should feel who, though in extremity, know that the word of the Lord endures forever. There are no richer hues than those of autumn. Though the leaves wither, shrivel, and turn to darkness and dust, they wear their brightest colors just before they die. The trees are not clothed in mourning, but in triumphal robes; in scarlet and gold, like kings. Do they not prefigure the deep and solemn joy which may invest and imbue the soul, the trusting soul, in the prospect of the last change? The trees cannot anticipate the new dress which they shall put on, when the warm influences of spring return the sap into their branches; but man may contemplate the season when "mortality shall be swallowed up of life"; the season not only of restoration, as to nature, but of inconceivable addition; the time when a new earth shall be under him, and new heavens over him, and glories of which he cannot now form any distinct conception, shall clothe the spirits of the redeemed.

"The grass withereth, the flower fadeth; but the word of our God shall stand forever." And let me ask whether it is not that very withering of the grass and fading of the flower which most effectually brings us to rest on the word of God? The conviction of frailty which is thus impressed upon the heart obliges it to inquire for that which is durable and unchangeable, and to seek for its security where alone it is to be found. While the green and glossy leaves stand thickly on the trees, we walk beneath them in shadow, and only see the earth, and the things which grow out of it; but when the leaves begin to fall, the light comes in, the view is opened upward, and we behold the ever blue and vaulted sky. The goodliness of man and his glory, are they not likewise apt to conceal the goodliness and glory which are above, infinitely above them? When they fade and are shaken down, a new radiance visits our eyes, the sunbeams shine in by day, and the moonbeams and starbeams by night, and heaven is revealed to the watching soul.

"The word of the Lord endureth forever: And this is the word," adds the apostle, "which by the Gospel is preached unto you." The word of God is spoken unto men. It is the word of life, light, and immortality, heard of old by but few and but partially, now published openly unto all; brought by Jesus, preached by his apostles, confirmed and sealed by his blood and by theirs; the trust, the comfort, and the joy of those who have believed in and followed them. The word of the Most High and Holy; his promise of the year which knows no blight or fall: this shall endure, though grass withers, and flowers fade, and hearts faint, and flesh fails, and the bodily forms and outward beauties and glories of men change and dry up and drop to the earth like autumnal leaves. This is the rock on which the spirit of man may lean amidst all temporal decays. God — heaven — eternity, — what else can be the sure rest of the soul? What is the grass, the flower, the leaf, that we should trust in them? What is their withering, their fading, their falling, that it should disturb our trust?

> " Let sickness blast, let death devour,
> If heaven must recompense our pains;
> Perish the grass, and fade the flower,
> If firm the word of God remains! "

OCTOBER 25, 1835.

SERMON XXIV.

IT IS WELL.

And she answered, It is well. — 2 *Kings*, iv. 26.

TOUCHINGLY submissive and full of pious trust was this answer of the Shunamite woman to the servant of Elisha. She had been seen by the man of God afar off, as she was coming, laden with her sorrows, to seek him; and he had sent Gehazi to meet her, and to inquire of her welfare and that of her family. The inquiries were, "Is it well with thee? is it well with thy husband? is it well with the child?" That child, the child of her age, her only child, had just died in her arms, and was then lying a corpse in her house. "And she answered, It is well."

A son had been given to her in her declining years, according to the promise of the prophet. He was sent to her and her husband, like a flower in winter, to cheer them with its unexpected fragrance and its late and delicate beauty. The shadows of life's evening had been slowly darkening the walls of their home, but now they smiled with an unwonted light; and the stillness which had settled over them was broken by the echoed gayety of childhood. Life had now for the parents a new object and a new purpose. They had a being to watch over, to provide for, to rear and educate, whom, by the strongest of bonds and the dearest of rights, they could call their own; — a being whose hopes and prospects gave them an unlooked-for interest in the future, and whose presence was as a constant memory of their own morning. It may well be supposed that such a family were seldom separated, and that the mother, especially, would hardly ever trust her child from her sight. But the time came when he must no longer be confined to the house, but, as he approaches toward manhood, be permitted to witness manly employments and labors. Still, however, if he occasionally quit one parent, it is only to place himself at the side of the other. If he leave his mother for a short season, it is only to take some message to his father in the field, or bear him pleasant company at his work. "And when the child was grown," says this simple and affecting history, "it fell on a day, that he went out to his father to the reapers. And he said unto his father,

My head, my head." A sudden illness had attacked him. Perhaps the hot sunbeams, as is not uncommon, had beat too fiercely on his young head. His father, not aware of his danger, merely gives orders that he shall be reconducted home. "And he said to a lad, Carry him to his mother." O where but to his mother shall the child be carried; and where shall he be safe from the smiting sun, and where shall his sick head rest and his fevered brain be quieted, and his pains be soothed and dispelled, if not on his mother's breast? But the blow had fallen too surely. The lad did as he was ordered. "And when he had taken him, and brought him to his mother, he sat on her knees till noon, and then died." "He sat on her knees till noon." Patiently, patiently did she hold him, watching his countenance as it grew paler and colder, and his eyes as they waxed more dull, till at last all hope was extinguished, and the child ceased to breathe.

And now that late, sweet flower is withered. The shadows fall deeper and darker than before on the Shunamite's house, since the spirit that was its light has been taken away. Where is now the father's solace at his toil? Who is there to go out to him while he is with his reapers? And who shall sit at home with the mother, beguiling her hours and improving his own, or kneel by her side while she implores the blessing of Israel's God? How lonely is their home! How aimless their life!

But the mother spends not her time in these repinings. She remembers the prophet Elisha. And she went up into the chamber which her hospitality had provided for him in her own house, and laid her dead son upon his bed, "and shut the door upon him and went out"; and equipping herself for the journey, hastened to the man of God to Mount Carmel, where he was at that time abiding. What the motives were which prompted her to this step, we are not assisted by the history precisely to tell. Perhaps she went only for counsel, encouragement, and sympathy. Perhaps, as her child had been in so remarkable a manner given to her, she went to ask why he had been taken away again so suddenly and so early, and whether any sin on her part had called down upon her the displeasure and chastisement of the Almighty. Or it may be that she cherished a hope, tremblingly and faintly, but fondly, which she would utter to no one, not even to her husband, that God would hear the prayer of his prophet, and restore to her the treasure which at the same intercession he had bestowed. But whatever were her hopes or intentions, her answer to Gehazi is proof that her mind was firm, collected, and resigned. "Is it well with thee?" said the messenger, in the name of his master; "is it well with thy husband? is it well with the child? And she answered, It is well." Her whole errand was not to be intrusted to the servant, but reserved for the hearing of the prophet himself. It was enough for her, at the time, to express her conviction that no real evil had befallen herself or her family. Gehazi no doubt understood her as meaning that she and hers were in health and prosperity. But there were far deeper meanings in her soul when she answered, "It is well." She knew that in the common and superficial sense of that phrase it was little applicable to her situation. She knew that her son was dead, and that her house was in mourning. But she felt that, in a holier and more thoughtful sense, the phrase was strictly suitable and true. "And she answered, It is well."

This is and always must be the answer of real piety in every providential affliction. It will be profitable to consider its import in connection with the circumstances of the above history, and analyze the thoughts which very probably were in the mind of the bereaved mother as she gave it utterance. Those thoughts may have taken a form somewhat like the following, while Gehazi, the servant of Elisha, stood before her.

"You ask me if it is well with me, with my husband, and with my child? Certainly it is well with us all. My child is dead. His beautiful features are fixed. When I kissed his pure cheek, it chilled me. These hands have closed his eyes. They no longer open on the light of day, nor rejoice in the lovely things of earth, nor look up to the blessed stars, nor do they reply any longer to mine. His sports and his walks are over. The dark tomb in the rock is ready for him, and there will his body be resolved into dust. And yet it is well with him. His spirit has returned to God who gave it, and even now communes with its Creator. He is safe; safer with his Father in heaven than with me on earth. How do I know that he may not have been taken away from some evil, some bitter evil to come, worse than the smiting of the sun by day or the moon by night; and that I, the mother who bore him, may not have had cause of more anguish in his life than I have now in his death? He is gone where there are no snares for innocence, no temptations to excess and disobedience, and where no foes can come. He must be safe, for he is in the dwelling-place of God. And he must be happy; happier than with me. It is true that his gentle heart had seldom throbbed, under my roof, with pain or fear, but had laid itself open to the influences of joy and peace, as a young heart should. Yet sorrows, which come to all hearts, must have come at last to his; and how do I know, blind as I am, how his might have been wrung? But where he is now, sorrows are not and can never be. God loved him, and therefore he took him wholly to himself, and to the pleasures and the glories which are forever springing up in the pathway of those whom he has led into his heavenly paradise. How can I dare to bring into comparison the joys which I here see to be so fading with those which there must be perennial; or lament that he, my darling and only son, should be removed from these to those? What they are, or where is the place of their growth, I cannot tell. Nor have our prophets told us much concerning them; for they can declare neither less nor more than is given them to speak. But my own soul tells me that the soul of my son lives, — lives with the souls of all saints, and with God the Maker of them all, in the light of whose countenance he cannot be otherwise than happy, beyond my power to imagine. Yea, it is well with him.

"And it is well with me. It is well with us, his parents, who expected, in the course of nature, to go before him, and not to have been left behind. We are stricken in years, but we have yet much to learn. It is good for us that we have been afflicted. It is well that we have been taught that the will of the Almighty is superior to the course of nature, and to be preferred to our own calculations and wishes. We are made to feel that we are strangers with him, and sojourners, as all our fathers were, and that the term of our pilgrimage and sojourn, and the time of our departure hence, are determined, and best determined, by his pleasure and not by ours. I am afraid that we had forgotten that our times were in his hand; and that our child belonged to him more properly than to us; and that the gift was not to divert our affections from the Giver, nor prevent us from considering that time and age were hurrying us away from all earthly delights into the immediate presence of the only Good. It is well that we have been reminded, though with seeming severity, of these great truths. For my own part, I am conscious that the nearer I was approaching to the end of my journey, the less I thought of its end, and the more unwilling I was to be brought to it. My son, though innocently, had stolen my heart from my God, who did not intend that I should take his precious gift, and turn it into an idol and worship it. I see this now, for my eyes have been opened. I feel it, for my heart has been dealt with. And it is well. It is well that I *can* see, and feel, and hear, and be instructed. It is well that my heavenly Father condescends to instruct me, even by chastening, and to cure me, even through suffering; for I feel, that, while his hand is heavy and sore upon me, it is, like that of a wise physician, healing me too. He has been twice gracious to me: when he gave, and now that he has taken away; let me say with our patriarch, Blessed be his name for both. It is well that I can say, Blessed be his name. It is well that I can render something to the Lord for all his benefits, and show him that I am not utterly regardless of them. It is well, I say, that I can render something to him, if it is only my submission, my wants, and my tears.

"It is well. If the Lord had not needed my child, he would not have sent for him. He was spotless, he was fit for the Lord's purposes, and therefore he has taken him to be his messenger. I am sure that he came as an angel to me; and if now he is wanted for some higher service, who am I that I should deny him to his Creator?

"It is well, in one word, because what has been done has been done by the Lord my God, and whatever he does must be right and good. There is evil enough in the world from the abuse of his goodness, evil enough is done by his disobedient creatures; but all that he does is and must be right and good. Our wild passions and rebellions, our murmurings and complainings, our vain regrets for things as vain, our prejudices, excesses, vices, omissions, and transgressions, these are wrong and evil; but the plain doings of God, and events and appointments of his providence, these must all be right and good, whether they be afflictive or joyful. My affliction certainly has come from him, and therefore it is right and good. Yea, it is well."

It was the will of God, as we learn from the history, that this woman should have her son restored to her through the prophet's intercession. But it was before this event that she uttered those few but expressive words of resignation. In similar sorrows of our own, we may not look for a miracle, which was peculiar to her case, but should rather imitate her resignation and adopt her words, which are always applicable to all cases, and may be received like balm into all wounded hearts. The miraculous restoration of life in an individual instance may confirm our religious faith, and help our submission, inasmuch as it shows that life and death are equally in the hands of God, and under his supreme direction. A miracle, however, cannot be an example, because in its nature it is a rare departure from a common and established course. But the spirit and words of resignation, of piety, of faith, are ever an example to all. With the Shunamite mother, all bereaved parents may answer, "It is well." And with far better reason than she had may all Christian parents adopt her words. Her child was brought back to a brief and uncertain life, again to suffer and again to die. Our Lord and Saviour Jesus Christ raised all our children to life eternal, in the hour when he took little children into his arms, and proclaimed that of such was the kingdom of heaven; and when he rose himself from the grave, he gave all believing parents the assurance that they should rise to meet their children again, and to part no more forever.

AUGUST 28, 1831.

SERMON XXV.

OFFICES OF MEMORY.

I remember the days of old; I meditate on all thy works.
Psalm cxliii. 5.

How bountifully gifted is man. He lives, not only in the present, but in the past and the future. The days of his childhood belong to him, even when his hair is white and his eyes are clouded; and heaven itself may open on his vision, while he is wandering among the shadows of earth, and dwelling in a tabernacle of clay. He may look back to the rosy dawn and faint glimmerings of his intellectual day; and forward, till his unchecked sight discerns the dwelling-place of God, and grows familiar with eternity.

The greater part of our mental pleasures is drawn from the sources of memory and hope; for, while hope is constantly adorning the future with her fresh colors and bright images, memory is as active in bringing back to us the joys of the past; and, though it is also her duty to introduce its pains, it is with the veil of time becomingly thrown over them, to soften the severity of their features, and render their presence not only endurable, but often soothing and welcome.

But I would not speak of the pleasures alone which these kind handmaids of our life are commissioned to procure for us. They hold instruction in their keeping; and if we will intimately and seriously converse with them, we may receive from their lips the lessons of wisdom and virtue. They are to be consulted on the real business, as well as the meditative delights, of existence; for what would be the excitement of labor without the encouragements of hope? and where could experience go for his treasures if the storehouse of memory should fail? I might compare these faculties to the valuable friends who are always found ready to minister to our amusement, and participate in our gayety, and equally ready to counsel our sober hours, and assist our emergencies with effectual help.

Let us give our attention, at this time, to the instructive voice of memory. Let us lend a careful ear to the moral of her tales. Let us, like the Psalmist, when we remember the days of old, hallow our reminiscences, by meditating on the works of God, by tracing the hand of a merciful Providence through the varied fortunes of our course. We all have joys, we all have sorrows, and we all have sins to remember.

I. The memory of joy reaches far back in the annals of every one's life. Indeed there are many who persuade themselves that they never experienced true pleasure except in the earliest stages of their career, who complain, that, when the hours of childhood flew away, they bore off the best joys of life upon their wings, leaving passion to be the minister of youth, and care to be the portion of manhood, and regret and pain to drag old age into the grave. I cannot sympathize in these gloomy views. I consider them as in a high degree unjust to the happiness which God has spread out liberally through every division of our days, and which can be missed or forfeited in hardly any other manner than through our wilful sins. But I do not the less share the visions and participate in the pleasure of those who love to retrace the green paths of their early years, and refresh their hearts with the retrospect of guileless innocence, of sunbright hopes, of delights that the merest trifle could purchase, and of tears that any kind hand could wipe away. How many scenes exist in the remembrance of each one of us, soft, and dim, and sacred, beyond the painter's art to copy, but hung up, as in an ancient gallery, for the visits and contemplation of our maturer minds. Mellowed they are, and graced, like other pictures, by the slow and tasteful hand of time. The groves through which we ran as free as our playmate the wind, wave with a more graceful foliage, and throw a purer shade; the ways which our young feet trod have lost their ruggedness, and are bordered everywhere with flowers; and no architecture that we have since seen, though we may have wandered through kings' palaces, can equal the beauty of the doors which our hands first learned to open, and of the apartments which once rang with the echoes of our childish glee.

Then there was joy in our hearts when we first began to take a part in the serious business of life, and felt that we were qualifying ourselves for a station, perhaps an honorable one, among our seniors. We were joyful when we won the prize of exertion, or received the praise and the smiles of those whose praise and smiles were worth to us more than any other reward. Joy was our companion when we first went out a little way upon the broad face of the earth, and saw how fair and grand she was, covered with noble cities, and artful monuments, and various productions, and the busy tribes of men. Joy came with friendship, and affection, and confidence, and the pure interchange of hearts and thoughts. And more than this, we were joyful when we were virtuous and useful; when we strove against a besetting temptation, and knew that our spirit was strong to subdue it; when we came out boldly, and denounced injustice, and defended the right; when we gave up a selfish gratification, and received a blessing; when we forebore to speak ill of a rival, though by so doing we might have advanced our own claims; when we dismissed envy from our bosoms, and made it give place to a generous admiration; when we forgave an enemy, and prayed from our hearts that God might forgive him too; when we stretched out a willing hand, to heal, to help, to guide, to protect, to save; in short, whenever we discharged an obligation, and performed a duty, and earned the approbation of conscience.

Let me not omit, in the enumeration of joys, the memory of our religious experiences and improvements. Let me not be so dull and cold-hearted as to pass by the hours which were consecrated to a close and filial communion with our Father in heaven; the hours when we felt the burden of mortality taken off, and our souls left light and free; when we breathed a better atmosphere, and saw with a clearer vision, because the air of another world was around us, and the clouds of doubt had vanished away. There have been seasons in the life of every Christian when he has perceived that a fresh beam of divine light has come in upon his soul, that he has acquired a new apprehension of the attributes and providence of God, and that he has taken another step in the path of a holy pilgrimage. Such seasons are sacred, and sacredly let them be kept, in the record of every heart.

I have mentioned some of the joys to which memory may point us. The recollection must not be barren of improvement. It will show us, in the first place, how beneficent our Creator has been to us in furnishing each age with its appropriate pleasures, and filling our days with a variety as well as a multitude of blessings. It will teach us to keep an honest account of our enjoyments, and to avoid the fault of those who minutely reckon up their pains and misfortunes, but ungratefully pass over the kind allotments of Providence. He who is faithful to the mercies of Heaven will not forget that he has tasted them, even though they may have been long resumed. He has once had them for his own, and that is enough to inspire him with gratitude for the past, and with trust in the continuance of his Father's love.

There is another moral which may be deduced from the remembrance of our joys. It is evident that they are not all of equal value, and that we must dwell on some of them with more complacency and satisfaction than on others. Now we shall find, if our moral taste is not entirely perverted, that the joys which afford the greatest delight to our memory are those which flowed in childhood from its innocence, and in after-life from our good deeds. The lesson is obvious. If we take pleasure in recurring to the innocence of our first years, let it be our watchful care to retain and preserve it; for it is not necessarily destroyed by knowledge, nor does it invariably depart at the approach of maturity. It is in continual danger, and it must be guarded with constancy. It is like a fountain, which springs up in a frequented place, and is immediately exposed to rude contamination and surrounding impurities; but we may build a temple over it, and keep it fresh and clear. A similar improvement may be made of the memory of our good deeds. We should use all diligence in adding to their store; for if they are now the most precious treasures of the soul, they certainly will not diminish in price when the common enjoyments of life are losing their relish, and its bustle no longer engages us, and the tide of our energies is fast ebbing away, and we only wait for the summons of departure. What solace is there to an aged man like the memory of his virtuous actions! What medicine is there so healing to his wasted, solitary heart! What ground of hope is there so sure to his spirit next to the mercy of his God and the intercession of Christ his Saviour! And what wealth would not many a sinner give to purchase that which the wealth of both the Indies is too poor to buy!

II. But it is time that I should change my subject, and come to a sadder theme. We cannot pass through the world without the experience of sorrow; and of this, as well as of joy, memory becomes the monitor. Here also she has a tale to tell of the days of old; for even innocent childhood is not exempt from grief, and many a cloud will rise to interrupt the brightness of its morning. So is it with every succeeding period of our brief day. We were born to sorrow, and our lot must be fulfilled.

And let us not complain that the shadows of sorrow return to haunt us, after the term of its actual existence is over. Why should they not be permitted the same license as the phantoms of delight? The laws of memory are impartial, and do us no more injustice than the laws by which the realities of our condition are dispensed to us. If our sufferings as well as our enjoyments are rightly ordered, why not the remembrances of both?

Whether we are led back more frequently to the bright or the gloomy passages of life, depends very much on the structure and tone of our minds, and the character of our present circumstances. It is to be observed, however, that in either case the transition is easy from what we are to what we were; that it is often made without any exertion or even volition of our own; and that things of the lightest consequence have the irresistible power of effecting it. A face which meets us for a moment in the street, an old tree, a piece of household furniture, a snatch of music, the sighing of the wind, may bring along with them a crowd of imaginations and scenes which had not visited our mind for years, and seemed to have gone forever.

> "In memory's land waves never a leaf,
> There never a summer breeze blows,
> But some long smother'd thought of joy or grief
> Starts up from its deep repose;
> And forms are living and visible there,
> Which vanish'd long since from our earthly sphere."

We all of us know best what our own calamities have been, and know best how often and how poignantly their memory afflicts us. Some bitter disappointment, perhaps, came along in the spring-time of our life, breathing on our young and flourishing hopes like the cold east-wind, and converted them into a heap of withered leaves, and covered our heart with a mildew, which, though time and the sun have acted upon it, is still felt there, in the returning fits of memory, in its melancholy dampness. Or perhaps we were doomed to undergo the torturing attack of severe disease, or casual pain; and we shudder when we recur to its agonies. It may be that we lost our property; that we were cruelly neglected by the world, or unaccountably forsaken by a friend; and the thoughts of these things trouble us in the midst of our calmest repose. But there is a thought, darker than any of these, and more common, too, with all of us, and more frequently crossing the minds of all with its sweeping shadow, — the thought of those who, though tenderly loved, were never valued as they ought to have been till they were removed from our sight, — the thought of that oppressive hour when the hand which had been so often warmly grasped in ours grew colder and colder as we held it, and that expressive countenance became fixed like marble, which even then was answering ours with a placid smile, — the thought of those who are gone from among us — the memory of the dead. I will not dwell more minutely on this remembrance. It would be cruel to do so. Perhaps I have already said too much on a subject which needs no description to bring it home most painfully to our bosoms.

Perhaps I have struck too harshly on a chord which a touch or a breath will cause to vibrate with intensity. Oh, how many simple words there are, and unnoticed things, which raise up sweet faces of past times before the eye of our spirit, and make our heart swell and throb, even in the press of the indifferent crowd, and the world does not know it, because outwardly we are calm, and we mix with its people, and pursue our business as they do!

The memory of our sorrows is fitted to exert a favorable influence on the character by softening it, and moulding it to the form of gentleness, and preparing it for the impressions of religion and piety. The memory of disappointment may give us a friendly warning in the season of extravagant expectation, and teach us to shelter our hopes more cautiously than we did before, lest they should meet with a similar blighting. The memory of sickness may arrest us in a course of heedless indulgence, and repeat over to us the history of our pains, and induce us to fall back into the safer path of moderation; or it may speak to us while we are in the innocent enjoyment of health and ease, and without rudely alarming us may kindly tell us how frail we are, and how dependent on the will of the Almighty. The memory of our lost friends has many solemn and affecting lessons to enjoin upon us. It may whisper to us a kinder treatment of those who are still left to us, and entreat us to avoid even a word or look which might inflict undeserved pain on those who are likewise mortal and of uncertain continuance. It will also bid us prepare to take our place with them in the grave, and so to cherish and imitate all that was good in them as to be found worthy of joining them beyond the grave in the mansions of eternal happiness.

III. It remains for me to speak of the memory of sins; which ought to be the saddest, and which may also be the most useful memory of all. It is a memory which addresses itself to every conscience, and to which none but a careless or a hardened conscience will refuse to listen with serious attention. Who will say that they have never committed sin, and therefore cannot be annoyed by its remembrance? If there be any such, they must be answered in the words of St. John, "If we say that we have no sin, we deceive ourselves, and the truth is not in us." It cannot be true that we have no sin. The most obstinate self-deception alone could induce us to maintain an assertion so easily refuted, and so contrary to all experience. What! Have we never wasted our time; never abused our faculties and privileges; never disobeyed, with full knowledge of the wrong, a commandment of God? Have we never raised expectations, and then idly or intentionally neglected to satisfy them, thereby causing disappointment and pain? Have we never failed to state the clear and open truth, through fear, or pride, or some other motive worse even than those? Have we never detained what was not rightfully our own; never taken an unfair advantage of our neighbor; never perverted the power of authority or love which has been placed in our hands, so that, instead of a refuge, it became a torment? Have we been guilty of no secret faults or crimes? But I will ask no more questions of this nature. Surely, we have sinned and done wickedly. Let us not aggravate our offences by denying that we have offended; but when memory repeats to our hearts the history of our misdeeds, let us receive the rebuke patiently, nay, even reverently, that we may be profited, perhaps saved.

If we have not repented of sin, it is the office of memory to lead us the first steps to repentance, by which we secure forgiveness and eternal life. It is her part to remove, with friendly solicitude, the veils with which we may try to cover our past misdoings. It is her part to dwell with anxious emphasis on those blots of former days from which we would gladly turn away our reflections. Oh that she may be suffered to persevere, with ever recurring efforts, till we are subdued by contrition and penitence, and sink down in humility and self-abasement before a merciful and pardoning God!

But have we repented of sin, and felt that we have been forgiven? Even then let memory come and tell again the history of error and disobedience. The recital will remind us of our frailty, convince us of our sinfulness; and we shall thus be put upon our guard against future acts of folly and rebellion. A shield will be given us against impending danger; a motive to increased precaution and vigilance. Beacon-lights will gleam out from the past, to guide our present course, and warn us of the old and sunken perils. In times of excitement, of delusion, of trial, when the enemies of our virtue and constancy are out upon us with their forces, and we waver in the conflict, happy will it be for us then if the memory of former guilt rise up and interpose itself between us and them, point to the melancholy consequences of defeat, and stimulate us to the victory. Good reason we shall have to render thanks to God, and ascribe to him the power and the praise, crying, "Not unto us, O Lord, not unto us, but to thy name give the glory."

Cherish the memory of your innocent and lawful joys, that you may be grateful, just, and contented; of your sorrows, that you may be kind to your friends, and careful of yourselves; of your sins, that you may be penitent, and humble, and watchful. And God grant, that memory may be the friend of your last days, and the soother of your dying bed!

JANUARY 1, 1826.

SERMON XXVI.

PEACEFUL SLEEP.

I will both lay me down in peace, and sleep; for thou, Lord, only makest me dwell in safety. — *Psalm* iv. 8.

WHEN the work of the day is done, and its record is written; when the sun has set upon whatever we have performed or neglected, suffered or enjoyed since his rising; when the deep shades of night have closed around us, and our wearied head demands its pillow, our natural aspirations are for peaceful sleep. Though our temples are not pressed by the weight of a diadem, yet, with the royal psalmist, our prayer will be for repose and protection; for a heaviness will be on our brows, of which we would fain be disburdened, and our conscious weakness will call for a Guardian, to whom it can resign itself securely. If we are human, we shall desire rest; and if we are considerate, we shall pray for it. We shall desire rest, — rest of body and rest of mind.

We shall long for sleep, and not for sleep only, but for peace.

How can my sleep be sweet, unless I lay me down in peace? Unless the spirit be composed, how can slumber come to my senses so softly, and refresh my bodily powers so completely as it should? Unless peace smooth my pillow, how can it be easy to my head? I must lay me down in peace.

I must be at peace when I lay me down, at peace with myself. My conscience, my free, unbribed, honest conscience, must tell me that the day which is past is yet not lost; that I have done some things in its course which will give me no pain to remember, and which my angel will not be ashamed to record; that I have learned somewhat which will tend to my improvement, or unlearned somewhat which has been tending to my injury. It must tell me, that, if I have labored, it has not been in the service of vanity, whose wages are nought, or in the service of sin, whose wages are death; that, if I have abstained from labor, it has not been to indulge a slothful habit, but to supply fresh vigor to thought or increased capacity for action. My conscience must tell me, that, if I have been tempted, I have resisted temptation; that, if I have been afflicted, I have not idly and ungratefully murmured and rebelled, but have bowed and submitted, and acknowledged the chastisement to be wise and kind and paternal. My conscience must faithfully tell me wherein I have offended against the laws of virtue and against my own soul; and when the accusation is brought, my heart must humbly acknowledge it, and prevent the flight of peace by sincere repentance. The spirit of God must bear witness with my spirit that my attachment to the things of the spirit is gaining confirmation; that my grasp on the things of earth is losing its earnestness and tenacity; that, as the past day has brought me nearer to the gate of death, it has given me a clearer and happier prospect of the region which lies beyond it. My passions must be still; the sounds of warfare or riot must not be heard in my bosom; the stings of remorse must not torment me; the suggestions of evil desires must not beset me; but reason must bear sway, and virtuous thoughts must occupy me, and gentle affections must move me; for I must lay me down in peace with myself.

I must also be at peace with others, when I lay me down. With those who lie down under the same roof with me, let me feel that I am at peace. Let not the ranklings of domestic discord corrode my heart, and postpone the hour of my repose. Let me not be sensible that I have wronged or grieved or intentionally offended, by act, by word, or by look, by heat or by coldness, any one of those whose happiness should especially be my happiness, and whose feelings should be clothed with a sacredness in my sight, such as the ancients attributed to their household deities. As I touch, in succession, each cord which connects me with those who are nearest, let me feel that it is sound and unworn, and in no danger of breaking. And with all those whom I am accustomed to meet in daily business and intercourse, let me be assured that I am at peace when I lay me down at night. I must look into the recesses of my breast as searchingly as I can; and if there be any envy, malice, jealousy, hatred, lurking among them, I must forthwith discharge my breast of such unpeaceful inmates and intruders. I must be conscious that love has presided over my walk and over my communications with my fellowmen; that my dealings have been liberal, my actions just, my deportment kind. If I have been injured, let me be prompt to pardon the injury; so that when by and by I pray that my trespasses may be forgiven, I may add with calmness, "as I forgive those who trespass against me." If my wrath has been burning, even for sufficient cause, let me know that it is now burnt out; that its last, lingering embers died before the last rays of the setting sun, and that the earliest dews of evening fell coolly upon its ashes. If I have enemies, let me know that the enmity is on their part, and not on mine; and that I have studied the things which make for peace; and that, as far as in me lies, I live peaceably with all men. With my family, with my friends, with my companions and neighbors, with the whole world, let me feel that I am at peace, so that I may lay me down in peace, and sleep.

And thus shall I be prepared for the blessed conviction that I am at peace with God. How can I lay me down in peace, and sleep, unless I am at peace with him? Has he not been my preserver through the day? If sleep descend upon my eyelids, does it not come, with every other good gift, from him? And through the following moments of the night, as they tread on each other's steps so silently and swiftly, is it not he, and he only, who keeps and defends me? What a gracious care is that which, while I sleep, is vigilant on every side of me, and, while I am unconscious, is providing me with fresh stores of mental and bodily strength. What a mysterious eye is that which follows my soul through the deepest glooms of oblivion, while my own eyes are fast closed, and my own senses have forgotten their office, and makes the night to be light about me, and creates security and day in the midst of peril and darkness. I know not what nor where I am in the hours of slumber, but I know that the Lord is with me, and that he only can watch and uphold my soul. Above all, then, I must be at peace with him when I lay me down to take my rest at night. I must experience the perfect peace of those whose minds are stayed on him. I must feel that the peace which I enjoy with myself in my own spirit flows from conformity with his spiritual laws established within me. I must feel that the peace which I cultivate with my fellow-men is the fulfilment of his will, which ordains mutual love and benevolence between the members of his great human family, and which was fully manifested in the life and commandment of his well-beloved Son. I must feel that all the peace which I can receive, or communicate, or experience, is in unison with the peace of God; and that the peace of God is the sanctification of all the peace of earth; and that all the peace of earth, unless it be thus sanctified, is without its highest blessing and richest crown. I must, therefore, place my love supremely on him; must direct my gratitude chiefly to him; must establish my trust finally and most firmly on him. I must look back on my day as spent in his sight, and as he would have it spent; and for every omission and for every transgression I must humble my soul before him, and seek his mercy by true penitence, that I may hear his forgiving voice, and be at peace with him. At peace with him, I cannot be at enmity with myself, or with aught that he has made and loves. Lulled by the full harmony of an all-consenting peace, I shall close my eyes and give up my soul into the hands of its Keeper, saying with the psalmist, "I will both lay me down in peace, and sleep; for thou, Lord, only makest me dwell in safety."

Day passes rapidly after day, and night after night yet more rapidly; — and then comes the night of death, and the sleep of the grave. When will they come? Name the season and the hour. No man can name them. Earthly days and nights are measured by the earth and the sun. In summer, the days are long and the nights are short, and in winter the days are short and the nights are long. We can name throughout the year, from experience of former years, and relying on the continuance of our revolving system, the very moment when the sun of each day shall bid that day farewell. But when the day of each one's mortal life shall end, and when the shades of death's dark night shall close in upon it, cannot be told by mortal tongue. We may only say that the day of some will be longer than the day of others; and that the night will fall suddenly on some, and on others slowly; and that some will be terrified, and others soothed by the gathering darkness; and that some will lay them down to the last sleep in peace, and others in great trouble, in anguish, in despair. So has it been, and so will it probably be. But the longest day will be very brief, and yet quite long enough for God's purposes, and man's probation; and when the night does come, it will almost always come — for so has God's providence ordained it — to eyes that are drooping, and a head that is weary.

Death is called a sleep. To the body it is a longer, deeper sleep, of which the grave is the bed. But sleep has dreams, and "in that sleep of death what dreams may come!" I know not, indeed, why the parallel between sleep and death may not be continued, and death be a dreaming sleep to the soul, a dim and half conscious state, to be followed by a full awakening. No one may assert positively that it is not. But if death has its dreams, will they not partake of the soul's character; and will they not be painful or pleasant as the soul went to its sleep in warfare or in peace? Whether it sleeps or is awake, however, certain it is — a most vital and solemn certainty — that it is in the presence of Almighty God, the Father of spirits, who knows it, who sustains it in being, and who will pronounce its doom. If there be a fear in the heart of a dying man that his soul may be forgotten and left by its Maker, — vain is that fear. If there be a hope in his heart, a desperate hope, that his soul may escape its Maker's scrutiny, and fall away into unsuffering nothingness, — as vain is that desperate hope. It cannot be lost, it cannot escape from him who made it, and surrounds and follows it, the Fountain of all being, and the Soul of souls.

That night will come; that sleep will come; and it is thou, Lord, only makest me dwell in safety. Ignorant I am when my day will close, but well I know, that, if I wish my sleep to be calm and my rising to be joyous, I must lay me down in peace. And my peace must be made up of the same materials which formed the peace of every preceding night, — of the love and the duty, the piety and charity of every preceding day. The memories of all obedience, and the effects of all penitence must unite in producing the solemn peace of my last evening. I must be at peace with myself, at peace with my neighbor, at peace with my God. There must be no war in my soul, no enmity with my brethren, and my entire hope and trust must be placed in my Saviour and in my God. Then, when the sun of my life sets behind the dark mountains, and that night has come to me which comes to all, I will not be depressed by its deepening shadows; I will not dread its gathering terrors; I will not shrink from the sight of my narrow bed; but "I will both lay me down in peace, and sleep; for thou, Lord, only makest me dwell in safety."

SEPTEMBER 18, 1836.

SERMON XXVII.

CHRIST WITH US AT EVENING.

Abide with us; for it is toward evening, and the day is far spent. — *Luke* xxiv. 29.

On the first day of the week, the same day on which Jesus arose from the dead, two of his disciples were journeying to Emmaus, a village about seven miles from Jerusalem. As they were on their way, talking earnestly and in wondering perplexity of the mournful events of the past week, and the exciting reports which they had heard that morning, Jesus himself drew near and walked on with them. They did not recognize their Master, for they had no expectation of meeting him at the time, and moreover it was not the intention of Jesus to make himself immediately known to them. "Their eyes were holden, that they should not know him." He inquired, on joining them, what it was which formed the burden of their conversation, and which seemed to be of so engrossing and saddening a character. The disciples, expressing their surprise at his appearing to be ignorant of the late transactions at Jerusalem, proceeded to inform him of the apprehension and crucifixion of Jesus of Nazareth, "a prophet mighty in deed and word before God and all the people," whom they themselves had followed as the promised Messiah, believing "that it had been he who should have redeemed Israel." It was now, they added, "the third day since these things were done," and they had just been "made astonished" by the asseverations of several of their company, who declared that the body of their Master was not to be found in the sepulchre where he had been laid, and that they had been told by angels "that he was alive."

When they had concluded their account, in which they exposed the conflict which was going on within them between their grief and their wonder, their disappointment and their surprise, and also manifested their inability to reconcile the sufferings and shameful death of their Master with the conceptions which they, as Jews, had formed of his dignity and glory as the Messiah of Israel, Jesus, still unrevealed to them, rebuked them as "slow of heart to believe all that the prophets have spoken," and asked them whether it was not in conformity with the prophetical writings, properly interpreted, that the Messiah should have suffered thus, as an entrance into his true glory. "Ought not," he said, "Christ to have suffered these things, and to enter into his glory?" And then, directing their attention to the real character of the Messiah, and reconciling humiliation and suffering with success and glory, "he expounded unto them in all the Scriptures the things concerning himself."

While he was thus unfolding, as no one else could have unfolded, the true and spiritual meaning of the holy writings, his words and manner exerted their accustomed influence over his disciples. Their hearts confessed a wonted power, and strangely "burned within them" with the glow of awakened sensations and memories. In this manner "they drew nigh unto the village whither they went; and he made as though he would have gone further." But they, anxious to secure more of the company and conversation of one who had so deeply interested them, urged him to stay with them, and adduced the lateness of the hour as an argument for his remaining, — saying, "Abide with us, for it is toward evening, and the day is far spent." Jesus consented, and "went in to tarry with them." And it came to pass, as he sat at meat with them, he took bread, and blessed it, and brake, and gave to them." Probably there was something in this usual act, and in the words which accompanied it, by which their Master was revealed to them. But in whatever way it was effected, "their eyes were opened, and they knew him." He then "vanished out of their sight"; leaving them to say to one another, "Did not our heart burn within us while he talked with us by the way, and while he opened to us the Scriptures?" That same hour they returned to Jerusalem, to relate what had taken place, and to confirm by their testimony the resurrection of their beloved Lord.

There is much in that evening scene between Jerusalem and Emmaus which we may profitably apply to our own hearts. Whenever the day is far spent, and the evening is coming on, we may join those two disciples in spirit, and adopt their words, and ask the Saviour of men to abide with us.

1. And, first, we may express this desire for the Saviour's companionship at the time of the natural evening. At that calm and holy time when the sounds of the world's business are ceasing, one after another, and the air is growing still, and our souls are insensibly disposed to harmonize with the time, and also to become quiet and still, whose company may we more fitly seek than that of the meek, peaceful, and sinless Jesus? During the day, it may be, while the sun was climbing up the

sky, and the race and contest of worldly pursuits and competitions were going vigorously on, our thoughts have been hurried into the midst of them, and in that turmoil have been excited and vexed, bewildered, and then fatigued even to exhaustion. But when the sun declines, and the fever of the strife is passing off, our thoughts are inclined to leave the crowd and enter into more green and solitary ways, that they may have a season of recovery and rest. Then it is that the Saviour, who is always ready to meet sober and prepared hearts, may join us, and walk with us; and then it is that we may induce him to abide with us. For the Master may abide with disciples even now, though not in the body, yet essentially, and as effectually as ever, in the influences which proceed from his life and character, and which join themselves to the souls which invite them. He abides with us when the model of his example is near to us and points out to us our duty. He abides with us when the thought of his love toward us, and his sufferings undergone for us, comes with power to our hearts, causing them to burn within us. He abides with us, really and truly abides with us, when his own spirit dwells with us, — when we feel that we sympathize with him in those pious sentiments which filled his breast, and those benevolent purposes which guided his course on earth,— when we enjoy the contemplation of his holiness, and are sure that we are made better by the contemplation. Thus it is that he abides with us. And how can we receive into our affections a more profitable guest? When the day is far spent, who, as he, can speak to us on the most wise and gainful use of our fleeting hours? Who, as he, can teach us to improve our daily opportunities, to dispose of our daily cares, to discern between the innocent and the hurtful, the true and the false, the right and the wrong? Certainly there is no one who can discharge as he can the office of instructor and friend, and prepare us by evening admonitions for morning watchfulness and daily work. Seriously and kindly he will inquire of us what we have done during the past day. If we have done ill, he will move us to repentance; if we have done well, he will crown us with his approbation. If we have done nothing, but have been standing all the day idle, he will incite us, by all those motives which are most prevalent with the better nature, to redouble our diligence for the days which may remain to us, in order that we may, as far as possible, repair our loss.

Let us call to mind some of the characters and accompaniments of the natural evening, and mark how the presence of Christ and his religion harmonizes with them and exalts them.

Peace comes with evening. It is a gentle and a soothing season. But the peace of Christ abiding with us will make it yet more peaceful; because it is the answer of the internal to the external; the quietness of the bosom rendering more profound and grateful the quietness of the atmosphere, of the land, and of the ocean; and because it alone can give security against the fears of darkness, the disturbances and alarms of night. It is a peace which corrects all that harshness of our humanity which is apt to disturb with its dissonance the repose of nature, or render us impenetrable to its influences.

The soft, broad shadows come with evening. They close round us as if they would envelop and shade the spirit, too much heated and wearied before, giving it time for restoration. But how much safer and more quiet is the spirit, if by the side of the Son of God it claims a higher protection, and takes refuge under the shadow of the Almighty.

The dews come with evening. They gather coolly on the drooping leaves, and stand in refreshing drops on all the panting flower-cups, and on every blade of grass; but it is only the Christian, only he who places his hope in

Christ, and with whom Christ is abiding, who can tell with what a reviving efficacy the dews of heavenly grace fall down upon the drooping soul.

The bright stars come out with evening. Splendidly they shine and solemnly — those mighty orbs, so far away that every beam from them, with all its swiftness, has required years for its journey hither; but with a more intelligent brightness will they shine if Christ be with us to lead our adoring thoughts to the Almighty Father, who feeds them with their light, and has prepared a place yet more elevated and more glorious than theirs, in which his redeemed children shall dwell with him forever.

Sleep comes with evening. But let us not lie down, as do the flocks and herds in the fields, without a prayer to him who sends us slumber; for we are capable of religion, and they are not. Sweetly will sleep fall upon our eyelids if we have been holding communion with our Saviour in heavenly-mindedness, and, as if we heard from him the words of kind permission, " sleep on now, and take your rest," we can commend ourselves in confidence to the Watchman of Israel.

2. The day, which was far spent when the two disciples stopped at Emmaus, was the day of our Lord's resurrection. It was the first

Christian Sabbath, the first Lord's Day. The associations which belong to that day, and the sacred observances to which it has been devoted, have made it the weekly Sabbath of Christians. Sabbath is rest. For its rest, for its silence, for its holiness, the Sabbath may be likened to the evening. It is the evening of the week. At this season, then, so especially consecrated to the Saviour, he may especially abide with us. Indeed we would meet him every day, and every evening we would ask him to abide with us; but on this evening of the week his abiding with us may be more than usually confidential and uninterrupted. Who shall interrupt it with the noises of the world? To break in upon the devotion of the Lord's Sabbath, and upon the repose which is connected with that devotion, with no plea but one's indifference or one's fancy, is as barbarous a thing, and as offensive to right feeling, as if the rude and hasty sounds of business were to be wakened up at nightfall, to rend and break asunder the calmness of eventide, and tramp and rattle through the offended darkness. One profanation is as great as the other. Let the evening of the week, as the evening of the day, be preserved in quietness, that we may commune with the Lord of this Sabbath, and he may expound to us the Scriptures, and abide with us in peace.

3. But there is another evening. This our life is called a day, and it has its evening, — which many of our race, however, are not permitted to see. It is when the sun, which rose on our birth, and glanced its morning beams on the hours of our childhood and youth, has passed the meridian of our short maturity, and now drops down toward the place of its setting, to rise no more in this world. The morning has passed away — how quickly! — with its early lights and fresh tints; and perhaps its promises and aspirations, like silver mists, have exhaled into the thin air. The hot passions and noontide turbulences of busy manhood are assuaged. The loud winds are lulled. Coolness, moderation, and repose, as they betoken the natural evening, so are they the signs of man's closing day. Old age is the evening of life.

And when this our own day is far spent, and the evening is at hand, shall we not desire that the Saviour may abide with us? Shall we not need his company in our solitariness; his conversation and instruction during the sober twilight season; his help in our weakness; his prayers for the approaching night?

Has he been with us through the day? Did our hearts seek him early, even in the morning; and have our advancing steps been guided by his counsel; or, if we wandered, did we hear his voice and return? If so, then we cannot now permit him to depart from us; but, having enjoyed his sacred fellowship thus far, we shall earnestly beseech him to abide with us to the end, and be more and more near to us, as the darkness falls faster around us. If we have experienced the happiness and safety of Christian faith in our past life, we surely cannot dispense with it when the joys of earth are becoming more few, and friends are dropping away, and our eyes are growing dim, and that last hour of the evening is drawing nigh when nothing but faith can yield a ray of light to our spirit, or put a staff into its hand, as it enters the valley alone. If Christ have journeyed with us in our youth and strength, — and happy may we be accounted if he have, — it is incredible that we should suffer him to leave us when the journey is almost accomplished and we are weary, helpless, and old.

But it may be that he has not journeyed with us in our youth and strength, and that our day, far spent as it is, has been spent without him and away from him. If this be our case, it is mournful, but not yet hopeless. The Saviour is still within hearing. The pardon and peace of the gospel may be found, though sought late, if they be sought sincerely and with deep penitence. Let us thus seek them in our decay, if we foolishly slighted them in our prime. Or do we, with a more marvellous folly, think that we cannot decay? Are we so blind and infatuated, that, while the hand on our life's dial points to threescore and ten, we will not be persuaded that the night is nigh? To see a young man without the beauty of religious feelings, principles, and hopes, is a sight of sufficient sadness; but to see an old man without its supports, consolations, and fruits, without holiness, without Christ, is truly deplorable. How can they, whose remaining moments are not many, refrain from seeking him immediately, imploring him to abide with them, and asking his neglected but still indulgent blessing on their gray hairs? Why will they not go to him at once, saying, " Friend of sinners! abide with us, for we have no help or hope but in thee and God; abide with us, for our day is far spent, our sun is going down, and the evening is darkly closing in!"

And yet not one half of those who are born into this world, my friends, see the evening of old age. And though we all did, it still would be our best wisdom to seek the Lord betimes, to make religion our early companion, and not to lose in folly, or abuse in sin, our morning and our noon. But the shadows often fall from the mountains before we look for them. The night of death often comes down suddenly, and unushered by the gradual evening. It is then our only safe course to engage the Saviour to abide with us constantly, as if it were always toward evening, and our own day were far spent. And while this course is the only safe, it is also the only happy one. A state of preparation is far from being a state of inquietude and gloom. It need not disturb one joy of life. It ought rather to enhance them all. Nor can there be any gloom where Christ truly abides. His presence disperses all terrors. Unhappy is he who prepares not, and postpones from time to time the security of the Saviour's companionship. It is he who is exposed to the terror by night, and the arrow by day. It is he whose condition is gloomy. When we know that death may be near at any moment, how can we suffer the Redeemer to be at any moment away from us? How can we think serenely of the impending night, if we have no interest in him who is the Light of men? How can we anticipate the sleep of the grave with any calmness if we have no hope of sleeping in Jesus, no trust that the morning of the resurrection will shine brightly on our waking eyes?— The night cometh; but when, we do not know. The disciple will, at all seasons, and through every hour, keep near to his Master. He will say to him, Abide with me always!—

> "Abide with me from morn till eve,
> For without thee I cannot live;
> Abide with me when death is nigh,
> For without thee I dare not die!"

JULY 15, 1832.

THE END.

www.ingramcontent.com/pod-product-compliance
Lightning Source LLC
Chambersburg PA
CBHW030006240426
43672CB00007B/847